THE IBERIAN STONES SPEAK

ARCHAEOLOGY IN SPAIN AND PORTUGAL

BOOKS BY PAUL MACKENDRICK

The Mute Stones Speak
The Greek Stones Speak
The Iberian Stones Speak

THE
IBERIAN
STONES
SPEAK

ARCHAEOLOGY IN SPAIN AND PORTUGAL

Paul MacKendrick

FUNK & WAGNALLS   New York

For D. G. M.

Foreword

THIS BOOK IS A COMPANION TO *THE MUTE Stones Speak* (New York, 1960) and *The Greek Stones Speak* (New York, 1962). Like them, it is an attempt to reconstruct cultural history from archaeological remains. Because so much that is fascinating about the archaeology of the Iberian peninsula is pre-Roman, there is more pre-classical material in this book than in the others; I have been at particular pains to emphasize the persistence of the Iberian tradition under Roman rule.

I am grateful to the American Council of Learned Societies, which taught me Portuguese in the summer of 1941, and to the United States Navy, which put my knowledge to use in Portuguese-speaking lands from 1942 to 1945. I regret that my visits to Spain and Portugal had to be made at times when working archaeologists were inaccessible; for this reason I am the more grateful to Professor Luis Pericot of the Universidad de Barcelona, Dr. H. Schubart of the Deutsches archäologisches Institut in Madrid, and the librarians of the Museo Arqueológico Provincial and the Museo de la Historia de la Ciudad, both in Barcelona; and of the Academia de Belas Artes in Lisbon. Readers will join me in thanking the University of Wisconsin Cartographic Laboratory for the trouble they took over the maps.

Madison, Wisconsin
October, 1968

vii

Contents

4

5

6

7

Illustrations

1

2

3

4

5

6

7

8

1

FROM THE CAVE MAN
TO THE
BRONZE AGE

(12000-1000 B.C.)

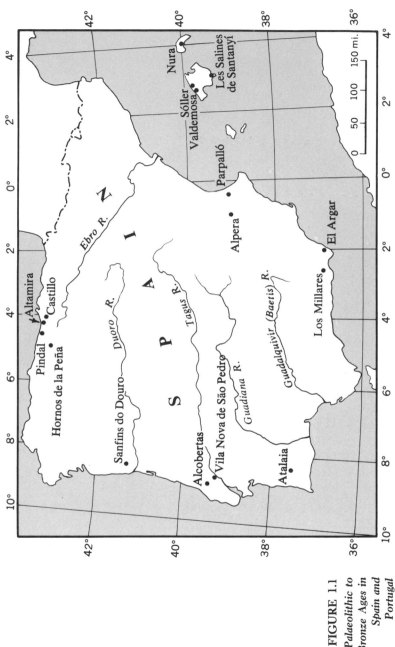

FIGURE 1.1
Palaeolithic to Bronze Ages in Spain and Portugal

ONE DAY IN 1879 DON MARCELINO DE SAN-
tuola, digging for prehistoric tools in front of a rock shelter near San-
tillana del Mar (Santander; see map, Fig. 1.1)* where he kept farm
implements, heard his little daughter Maria cry from inside the cave,
"Toros! Toros!" He squeezed in and found her with a lighted candle,
looking up at the ceiling at what the world now knows as the cave
paintings of Altamira (Fig. 1.2), once described as "the Sistine Chapel
of Palaeolithic art."

Maria's "toros" were bison (Fig. 1.3), but among the 150 animals
on the cave ceiling, crowded into the darkest corner, and often super-
posed, in a space of about 30 by 60 feet, there are also horses, a
huge stag over seven feet long (Fig. 1.4), ibex, boar, elk, and wolf. The
paintings are done with the utmost liveliness and realism: the bison
are rendered not only proudly standing, but bellowing or at full gallop,
their legs gathered up under them; the drawing is so accurate that experts have been able to identify the species.

The artist was complete master of his medium. His strokes are bold
and clear, in spite of the irregular surface on which he worked; he took
advantage of the protuberances or bosses on the cave ceiling to show
relief, and he used foreshortening and chiaroscuro. His colors are red,

---

* Throughout the book, the province or (in Portugal) *concelho* in which a
site lies is shown in parentheses.

FIGURE 1.2
*Altamira, ceiling of cave showing use of protuberances
to give the paintings relief*

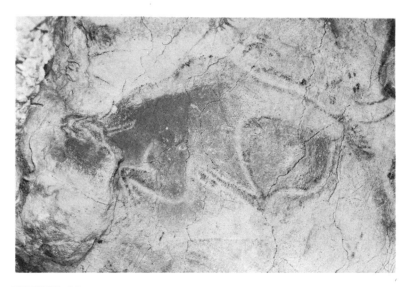

FIGURE 1.3
Altamira, cave painting: galloping bison

yellow, brown, violet, and black, for which he used ocher—lumps of it were found on the cave floor—hematite, manganese, and vegetable carbon.

Bones of the animals portrayed were also found on the cave floor, and stone tools of the period called Upper Magdalenian, whose absolute date is about 12000 B.C. It is astounding and improbable, but true, that our ancestors over 400 long generations ago were capable of creating works of art which need not fear comparison with anything achieved since. "Primitive" is hardly the word for the culture which produced the Altamira paintings; thus at the very outset Iberian archaeology induces that sense of perspective, proportion, even humility, which is one of archaeology's great rewards. We come to recognize a little better our place in space and time, to be a little more careful about using "modern" as a word of praise and "ancient" as one of scorn; even to recognize "modernity" wherever, as at Altamira, there is evidence of the vital spark of creative genius.

The genius is all the more remarkable because of the difficult conditions under which the artist must have worked. He had only a flint tool to incise his outlines; his brush was a tuft of hair, or feathers, or

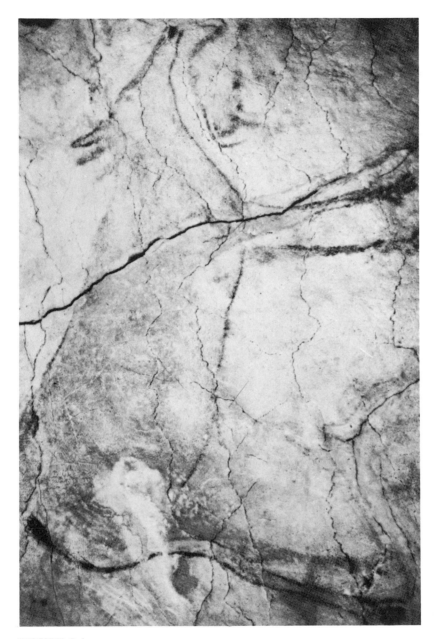

FIGURE 1.4
Altamira, cave painting of huge stag

FIGURE 1.5

*Pindal (Asturias),
cave paintings of
mammoth with
heart marked like
bull's-eye. Repro-
duction, Museo
Arqueológico
Provincial, Bar-
celona*

twigs; he applied his paint mixed with heated grease or resin. He had to work by artificial light, and in an awkward position, for in some places the cave roof and its floor are only a little over a foot apart. Why should he have spent his talent in a dark corner of an almost inaccessible cave? A plausible answer came when, in caves found later, archaeologists discovered the animal figures riddled with arrow marks. The artist was making sympathetic magic to make the hunting good. Another excellent example, from the cave at Pindal (Asturias), portrays a mammoth with the heart marked like a bull's-eye (Fig. 1.5).

Santuola published his findings, locally and modestly, in 1880. His interest stimulated by prehistoric objects he had seen in the Paris Exposition of 1878, he decided to explore his own province, to try to tear away the thick veil that obscured understanding of prehistory, and, as he says with charming diffidence, to prepare the way for more competent persons. He records what he found on the cave floor: shells of scallop and snail, bones engraved or pierced for use as awls, animal teeth, horn, river pebbles split for use as hand axes, bits of handsome, gleaming rock crystal which must have appealed to the same nascent aesthetic sense which inspired the art. Anticipating skepticism, he admits that the paintings are so well preserved that it is hard to believe they are ancient, but he points to the lumps of red ocher found on the cave floor and reminds his readers that though these are the first cave paintings ever discovered, competent drawing on stone was already known. Some may deny the existence of bison here so long ago, but he appeals to the authority of the great French naturalist Buffon, and remarks that the question will be settled—as it later was—if the cave yields bones of the animals painted. Some, he says—and he was a true prophet—will think this the work of some new Apelles, but the cave was unknown until a few years ago, and why should a modern artist paint animals now extinct in the region? He concludes, sensibly, that the paintings are Palaeolithic, and expresses his satisfaction that they have been discovered and will be protected.

His satisfaction was short-lived. The nineteenth century was the age of the Higher Criticism, and skeptical professors—with one notable exception in Madrid—ignored or scoffed at his remarkable find. A prehistoric congress in Lisbon in 1880 paid no attention to it, in 1881 the allegation was made that the paintings had been done between 1875 and 1879; a French scholar in 1883 attributed them to Spanish Jesuits intent upon discrediting the new science of prehistory, which placed the creation of the world uncomfortably early. Santuola died in 1888, without the satisfaction of seeing his discovery accepted in learned circles.

The tide turned in 1901, with the discovery of exactly similar cave paintings at Font de Gaume, in the Dordogne. (Lascaux, discovered in 1940, is even more spectacular than Altamira, but it is now closed to the public, whereas Altamira may still be visited, and there are replicas of it in the Deutsches Museum in Munich and under the garden of the Museo Arqueológico Nacional in Madrid.)

In 1902 the distinguished prehistorian Émile Cartillac handsomely retracted his previous rejection of the genuineness of the Altamira paintings, and in the same year he, with a colleague, received a grant to study and copy the paintings. The colleague was one of the fascinating "characters" who enliven the history of Iberian archaeology, the Abbé Henri Breuil. He never had a parish; his Church recognized the vocation of his one-track mind, the joy he took in touching with his own hands our remotest ancestors. Late in life he wrote: "Limitless love of truth is a fundamental disposition of the mind, without which no human life, religious or scientific, is worthy of the name. This is the principle which has guided my steps, and which I have never had to violate, either to remain a convinced Christian or to serve science with an enthusiasm which still sustains me." His admiring students have recorded how gladly, in pursuit of palaeolithic man, he would live in smugglers' smoke-filled cabins, ride mule-back across rocky hillsides, wade and dive in icy streams to see a 20,000-year-old cave bear. He first visited Portugal to study prehistory in 1916. Arrested as a spy, he was allowed to work under surveillance; his guard carried his finds for him. He was finally cleared by the great Portuguese prehistorian Leite de Vasconcelos. The anecdote reflects credit upon the Portuguese character as well as upon his own. He had a fine aesthetic sense about prehistoric craftsmanship. Asked to classify the finds in the Museo Geológico in Lisbon, he replied, "My friend, this material is without interest; the men who made it worked like pigs!" His life (1877–1961) spanned half the course of modern scientific archaeology; he lived in its Heroic Age; and he died the unquestioned and autocratic dean of Palaeolithic studies. He worked at Altamira by candle-light, lying on fern-stuffed sacks. The beautiful water colors which resulted were published through the munificence of Prince Albert of Monaco in 1906 and again, even more sumptuously, at the expense of the Duke of Alba, in 1935. The result was that Altamira became world famous. The King of Spain visited the cave in 1920; in 1924, at the Exposition of Prehistoric Art in Madrid, special tribute was paid to Santuola at a meeting fittingly presided over by the original discoverer, his daughter Maria.

Though blasting in a quarry above the cave damaged the ceiling and let in water, the Duke of Alba subsidized repairs by the injection of liquid concrete. Electric reflectors were installed, the humidity was kept constant (a difference of three percent turns the paintings gray) and the temperature maintained at a steady 61.2° Fahrenheit. Thus the conditions which forced the closing of Lascaux were at Altamira avoided, and it remains open to inspire the visitor with a sense of the millennial achievements of the human race.

Altamira is far from being the only prehistoric site in the Iberian peninsula; it is only the most interesting. Between 1908 and 1935 the Abbé Breuil published no less than 267 articles on sites in southeast Spain (the "Spanish Levant"). He suggested to Luis Pericot, now the well-beloved dean of Spanish prehistorians, an excavation of the cave of Parpalló (Albacete), which Breuil had known since 1913, but had been prevented from digging by the First World War. Pericot began work there in 1929, but was prevented by administrative chores (the professor's curse) from publishing his results until 1942. The spot is attractive, in a valley 1,750 feet above sea level, some seven miles northwest of Gandía, off the main coast-road from Valencia to Alicante. Almond trees flourish there, and the olive and the vine, carob trees, pines, lentiscus, esparto grass (for basket weaving), and the palm. Breuil was not its first discoverer; that honor goes to a geologist of 1872, out on a field trip with a pupil. They found the cave so rich in prehistoric stone tools that they soon had too much for a pack animal to carry. There was further exploration in 1893 by Vilanova y Piera, the Madrid professor who had stood alone against the learned world in his belief in the antiquity of the Altamira paintings. The local inhabitants believed the cave contained a treasure. (Spanish peasants are invariably convinced that all archaeological sites have something to do with treasure, or the Moors, or, preferably, both.)

FIGURE 1.6
Parpalló (Albacete), plaque incised with doe

On the very first day of his excavation, Pericot found an engraved plaque, of the kind mentioned by Santuola in his 1880 article. These plaques were the prehistoric artist's sketch blocks. A drawing of a hind on an animal's shoulder blade, found at Altamira, is matched line-for-line by another from Castillo, in the same province (Santander). At Hornos de la Peña (Santander) a sketch on bone of a horse's hindquarters is matched by another on the wall. In France the sketch and the finished product have been found in places 200 miles apart. Pericot found that there had been a veritable "school" for artists at Parpalló; he unearthed no less than 1,430 such plaques. The subjects are animals (Fig. 1.6): a doe suckling a fawn, stags, goats, horses, bulls, boars; as at Altamira, the same animals whose bones littered the cave. He does not believe, however, that these drawings were sympathetic magic; they simply indicate the caveman's delight in draughtsmanship. It is provincial work, rather document than art; what matters more is that Pericot managed to record at Parpalló a clear stratification—something regrettably rare until recently in Spanish archaeology—going down over 20 feet and distinguishing tools running back from Magdalenian IV to Upper Aurignacian, with absolute dates of *ca.* 25000–12000 B.C. In his lowest levels, Pericot found the finely worked figure-eight-shaped stone blades which he recognized as Aurignacian; above this, fine Solutrean stone spearheads, shaped like a laurel leaf; closest to the surface, the tiny arrowheads (microliths) characteristic of Magdalenian culture. (The names come from findspots in France, where scientific prehistorical studies first developed.) One piece of negative evidence interested him. He found none of the backed blades or geometric-shaped implements, crescents and triangles, characteristic of Capsian culture (named for the oasis of Gafsa, in Tunisia). This meant that, at the time the Parpalló cave ceased to be inhabited, there was as yet no North African influence on the Palaeolithic culture of southeast Spain.

In rock shelters or niches, shallower than caves, in the Spanish Levant, archaeologists have found paintings. These are crude but lively impressionistic stick figures of men—for the first time in art—and animals, much inferior in execution to the Altamira masterpieces, but striking. (Professor Pericot has had reproductions of them made into slipcovers for his study.) They are done in a red or black glaze (the binder being blood, honey, albumen, or vegetable juices) on a gray base. Seepage of water with a high calcium content preserves them,

FIGURE 1.7

Alpera (Albacete), cave painting of stag-hunt. Reproduction, Museo Arqueológico Provincial, Barcelona

much as the calcium hydrate in mortar preserves a fresco. They are small scale, usually hunting scenes (of animals who do not love the cold, such as the red deer, goat, ibex, ox, boar, wild horse, elk, or chamois), but there are also a mother and child, men in animal masks, a spider, and flies. The men wear breeches, fringed capes, armlets, beards, and moustaches; the women wear bell-skirts and are barebreasted. In one animated scene of a stag hunt from Alpera (Albacete) of which there is a copy (after Breuil) in the Museo Arqueológico Provincial in Barcelona (Fig. 1.7), the tallest figure wears a feather headdress and is obviously a chief. He forms part of a frieze 33 feet long, with 75 animal and 16 human figures. Since the hunters use bows and arrows, unknown to Magdalenian peoples, these paintings are obviously later, and belong to the Mesolithic Age, which in Spain is dated between 10000 and 5000 B.C. Since paintings very like these are known from Africa, it is now thought that it was in Mesolithic times that African influences began to reach Spain across the Straits of Gibraltar, even narrower then than now.

Not many Neolithic Spanish sites have been published, but one on the island of Mallorca has the advantage of carbon 14 dating. Some bones of the antelope-gazelle, a small animal (it would have weighed about 35 pounds) related to the Rocky Mountain goat, found in a cave on the north coast, off the strikingly beautiful road between Valldemosa and Sóller, have been dated at 5184 B.C. ± 85 years. The animal was trapped along with its human owner (evidence for the early domestication of animals) by a rock-slide, a tragedy which preserved the remains until this day. The island is 115 miles from land, but the lower sea level in the last glacial period made access easier. By now man had learned to make pottery, and some unique thin-walled red-brown burnished ware rewarded the archaeologists. Other gazelle bones, dated at 3984 B.C. ± 109 years, give an idea of the millennial extent of Neolithic culture in the Balearics.

The Iberian peninsula is rich in metals, including copper. The copper mines near Los Millares (Almería) were exploited as early as 2345 B.C. ± 85 years (carbon 14 dating); Los Millares is the type site for the culture called Chalcolithic, transitional between Neolithic and Bronze. The original excavators, in the 1880s, were, as often in Spain, amateurs, a young pair of Belgian mining engineers called Siret, who excavated in their spare time and became experts on the Los Millares

FIGURE 1.8
Typical slate "idol-plaques," engraved with geometric designs

FIGURE 1.9
Alcobertas (Estremadura, Portugal), dolmen transformed into Christian chapel

culture. Digging was resumed, more scientifically, by Almagro and Arribas in 1953–1957. Los Millares was a fortified town (of which four towers and a stretch of wall with huts against it have been excavated and dated by carbon 14 to 2340 B.C. ± 85 years) with a necropolis (100 graves) which yielded rich finds: copper and stone tools and weapons, clay plaques, and figurines apparently of a Mother Goddess. Most characteristic are thin slate "idol plaques," engraved with geometric designs; they are found not only in the Spanish Levant, but in south and west Portugal (Fig. 1.8). This is also the culture of megaliths: beehive-shaped chamber tombs, corbel-roofed, set in a circular mound, and entered through a stone passage. These are sometimes called dolmens. (The word is Breton, and means a stone table.) The tomb chamber is made of huge stone slabs, sometimes weighing 65 to 100 tons, set on end and capped with other stones equally monstrous; the approach to the chamber is by a narrower stone passage, sometimes having several thin slabs with porthole-like apertures set at

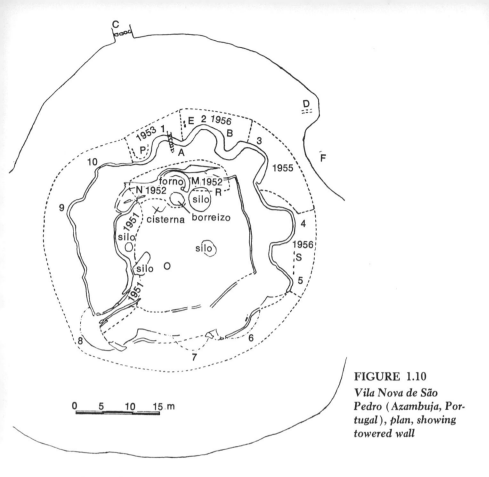

FIGURE 1.10

Vila Nova de São Pedro (Azambuja, Portugal), plan, showing towered wall

intervals along it. They are cruder examples of the tholos or beehive tombs, familiar to archaeologists, from the Mesará in Crete and from Mycenae.* They are especially abundant in Portugal (Fig. 1.9); many were published by the indefatigable German prehistorians George and Vera Leisner, but many more are quite unknown to scholarship. In a single afternoon at Sanfins do Douro, 12 miles east of Vila Real, a local archaeological amateur, Maurício Meireles Penha, showed me the remains of no less than ten. A third characteristic of this culture is a red-brown burnished and incised pottery drinking cup called the bell-beaker, which may have originated in Spain; the earliest examples at Los Millares are dated about 2100 B.C.

One of the most carefully excavated sites in Portugal contained copper and bell-beakers in the upper of its two levels. This is Vila

* See *The Greek Stones Speak*, pp. 68–71, 111.

FIGURE 1.11
Vila Nova de São Pedro, wall

Nova de São Pedro (Azambuja; Fig. 1.10), on a neck of land 328 feet above sea level, some 4 miles northwest of Cartaxo, which in turn is 42 miles north of Lisbon. Its most striking feature is a strong undulating wall (Fig. 1.11), in plan like a nine-leaf clover. A very similar wall, at Chalandriani on the Aegean island of Syros, is dated 2400–2200 B.C.; Vila Nova is a small Aegean town transported to Portugal. The Vila Nova wall was revetted with adobe on its outer face, and showed signs of burning on the inner. The excavator, Lt.-Col. Afonso do Paço, limited to short campaigns by military duty and shortage of funds, has been digging on the site since 1937. In spite of the partial destruction of his painstakingly stratified levels by treasure seekers and careless tourists, he has managed to record in print the precise findspots of most of the objects from Vila Nova now on display in the Museo do Carmo in Lisbon. The inhabitants lived in round huts, tattooed their faces (he found the tattooing needles and a clay plaque which he thinks may represent a tattooed face), dressed in linen (he found flax seed), and lived on grain (which they ground in stone handmills), vegetables, and meat (he found wheat-seeds, barley, acorns, vetch, beans, plums, and pine—the pine nut is delicious with wild boar—and the bones of the boar, hare, ox, goat, sheep, stag, porcupine, tortoise, wolf, bear, lynx, and beaver). At some stage, perhaps not the earliest, the Vilanovans domesticated animals. He found the bones of dog, horse, and mule. It was an industrial community. He found molds for copper-casting and slag in some of the houses. (There is no copper nearby; it must have come from the mines in the Alentejo.) The women used copper spirals for earrings. There was a pottery kiln (*forno*) against an inner face of the undulating wall. But they still used stone arrowheads, some in rock crystal, of beautifully delicate workmanship and in vast quantity; he found over 5,000. Combining the evidence of the arrowheads, the grain seeds, and the burning, he assumed a fight to defend a granary. Bone objects included punches, spatulas, pins, needles, a knife handle (with the copper blade attached), and small bone jars for cosmetics with traces of the cosmetics still inside. Clay plaques were crudely incised with sketches: bulls, stags, a doe giving suck, radiate suns, a bow, what he calls a hut (but it might represent either a dolmen or a Portuguese man-o'-war jelly fish), a clay idol with a representation of the female sexual triangle. The excavation is a remarkable achievement when one considers that it was operated with a handful of workmen (the budget averaged about 100 escudos—$2.80 or £1.3.4—a day), and the arrival of two Décauville cars and 50 meters of track in 1946 "*modificou totalmente o ritmo das escavações.*"

The early Bronze—as opposed to Chalcolithic—Age on the peninsula has as its type site El Argar (Almería), excavated, like Los Millares, by the Sirets. Argaric sites are generally on impregnable hills and have defensive walls and rectangular stone houses with cist-burials under the floors. Fine Microlithic arrowheads and cult figurines are absent; the tools and weapons are of coarse bronze, which means that Argaric peoples had access to tin to make the alloy. Argaric peoples settled Mallorca about 1500 b.c.; the evidence is, as usual, the pottery. The full Balearic Bronze Age begins about 1200–1000 b.c. What distinguishes it is the *talayot*—a local word for a small, strong-walled settlement—whose individual buildings look very like Sardinian *nuraghi* * and indicate some sort of contact—it is uncertain in which direction it ran—between Sardinia and the Bronze Age Balearic settlement. Figure 1.12 is a model, in the Museo Arqueológico in Barcelona, of a typical talayotic building, this one from Les Salines de Santanyí (Mallorca). Sometimes in a talayotic village several houses

---

* See *The Mute Stones Speak*, pp. 14–18.

will be surrounded by a secondary circuit wall, perhaps separating one clan from another. Olive trunks served as roof beams; sometimes a spiral staircase runs between the two faces of the wall, somewhat as in the Sardinian *nuraghi* (compare the place-name Nura on Menorca); at Nora on Sardinia graffiti written by Spaniards in the Iberian alphabet have been found. Especially on Menorca, there are handsome ship-shaped stone buildings called *navetas*, massively built without mortar. The inward-sloping walls are often over a yard thick. The entrance passages have port-hole entrances, as at Los Millares. Also on Menorca occur *taules* (the local word for tables), T-shaped monuments made of two monoliths, surrounded by a horseshoe of stones. The tombs now yield bronze axes, swords, spear points, chisels, bracelets, and bronze ingots, which indicate commercial contact not only

FIGURE 1.12
Les Salines de Santanyí (Mallorca), talayot, model, Museo Arqueológico Provincial, Barcelona

with Sardinia, but with Italy and the Aegean. German excavators at Atalaia in south Portugal have revealed Bronze Age tumuli of about 1500 B.C., with honeycomb additions unique on the mainland, but with parallels in the Balearic Islands, Sardinia, the Lipari Islands off northern Sicily, and on Leucas in the Adriatic. The largest central tomb will have been the patriarch's, with his lesser clansmen buried around him; we have seen this evidence of clan structure already on Mallorca. The Balearic Islands had become ports of call on a metal route; there are no mines on the islands. The finds are very rich, richer than the soil could have supported. Perhaps the men of Mallorca and Menorca had already begun, as early as the end of the second millennium before Christ, to go into foreign service as mercenaries, as later their expertise as slingers was to help make Carthaginian Hannibal's name one for Roman nurses to frighten their children with, and as still later their service with the Roman legions was to contribute to the long sanguinary story of the subjection of their own countrymen on the mainland.

2

SHIPS TO TARSHISH

(11000–500 B.C.)

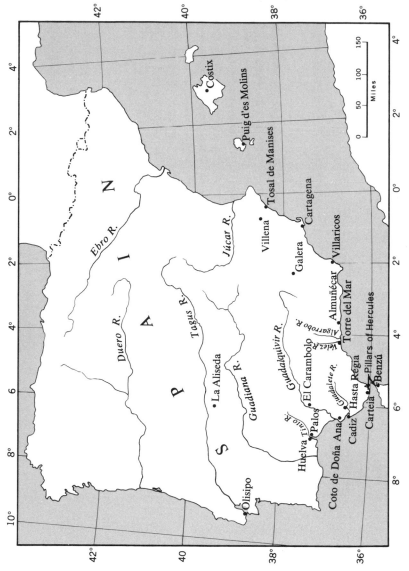

FIGURE 2.1
*Tartessian and
Punic Spain*

ONAH, BEFORE HE WAS SWALLOWED BY THE whale, had been traveling on a ship to Tarshish. From Tarshish, in Solomon's reign (973–933 B.C.), came ships "bringing gold, and silver, ivory, apes, and peacocks." This fabulously rich and exotic city (Tartessus in Greek) was somewhere in southern Spain, and archaeologists have spent a good deal of sweat, in vain, trying to find it.

The hardest worker was another foreigner, a German this time, who, like the Abbé Breuil, felt the fascination of Spanish archaeology and devoted half a lifetime to it. His name was Adolf Schulten; we shall meet him again when we discuss Numantia. In 1919 he did exploratory surveys in the hunting country at the mouth of the Guadalquivir River, north of Cádiz (see map, Fig. 2.1), not far from the present American base at Rota, tramping for eight hours at a stretch across the shifting sand dunes, ignoring both stifling heat and pouring rain. He found nothing. In 1922 he returned to Coto de Doña Ana, where he stayed in the Duke of Tarifa's hunting lodge and hit upon Roman walls, which he persuaded himself might contain blocks from Tartessus in re-use. The work was plagued by water seepage, which resisted the strongest pumps. In 1923 he found a bronze ring of a style datable to the sixth century B.C., when Tartessus was flourishing. It was inscribed in Greek, "Wear me with luck." It was the closest he ever came to finding Tartessus.

In 1926 he bored seven meters down with a geological drill (as was done with more success at Sybaris in south Italy), but found no trace of the elusive city. He went to his grave (he died in 1960) disappointed in his hope of becoming the Schliemann of Tartessus. His disappointment was exaggerated, for though the city has not been found, the culture has, and the ring is only one example of it.

But archaeologists are a stubborn lot, and the search for Tartessus still goes on. Some of them think it lies under the city of Jerez de la Frontera (the ancient Hasta Regia) where the sherry comes from, where excavation has uncovered pottery of the early Bronze Age (which might be called Tartessian) and after, including Punic amphorae like that from Puig d'es Molins (Menorca; see below) and Campanian ware from south Italy, dated in the third and second centuries B.C.

Others would locate Tartessus near Huelva, at the mouth of the Rio Tinto. The Rio Tinto runs red from the copper ore which has been mined upstream since antiquity, and copper was one of the major sources of Tartessus's wealth. (From Palos, on its left bank, Columbus sailed in 1492 to search for another El Dorado.) At Huelva, appropriately enough off the pier of the Tharsis Copper Co., dredging in the spring of 1923 dislodged an ancient wreck which proved to contain a large number of the products of Tartessian industry: over 400 bronze weapons—swords, daggers, and spear points—plus needles, fibulae (the ancient safety-pins), and buttons, which the experts date about 750 B.C. (Since swords of identical pattern turn up in the Balearic Islands, the Talayotic culture is plausibly thought to be of about the same date.)

In the summer of 1967 an American team, hunting for Tartessus, excavated at Carteia, near Algeciras, across the harbor from Gibraltar (still noted for its apes, and apes were a part of the cargo of the ships from Tarshish) but they found nothing earlier than the third century B.C., 200 years after Tartessus was destroyed.

So Tartessus still eludes us, but things made there, or under its cultural influence—which stretched all the way across the Southern Iberian peninsula—continue to turn up. In the autumn of 1963 in Villena, 36 miles northwest of Alicante in the Spanish Levant, a gypsy workman gave to his foreman, in the belief that it was a part of the gear assembly of a gravel truck, a gold bracelet he had found in a gravel pit. It took five weeks to get behind the natural gypsy deviousness and discover the true findspot in a stream bed three miles north of the town. A lucky blow of a pick struck a large basin containing a treasure; it had narrowly missed being crushed by the gravel trucks. The 60 pieces of gold, weighing nearly 20 pounds, included 28 bracelets, 11 bowls (in *repoussé*, the ancestor of Roman "Arretine" pottery), five bottles, two brooches, and a ring (Fig. 2.2). There were also objects in silver, amber, and iron (treated as a precious metal and therefore very early in date, perhaps 1000 B.C.). The experts call the period of the treasure "Late Argaric Bronze III"; the find is now in the Villena museum, giving mute but handsome evidence of the high level of Tartessian culture, a crystallizing in the West of a stimulus from the Greek East, induced in the second millennium before Christ by the search for metal.

In September 1958, in a clay-pigeon shooting ground at El Carambolo near Seville, was discovered another Tartessian treasure, this time of 21 pieces, weighing between six and seven pounds. It included gold bracelets, rectangular plaques, and a gorgeous pectoral of the "orientalizing" style prevalent about 600 B.C. (Fig. 2.3)—a similar example

FIGURE 2.2
Villena (Alicante), gold treasure as found

FIGURE 2.3
*Seville, Museo
Arqueológico
Provincial, gold
pectoral from
El Carambolo
treasure*

from Caere in Etruria is one of the treasures of the Vatican Museum.*

How do archaeologists connect treasures like these with Tartessian culture, when they cannot find the city which they allege produced them? Archaeologists cannot make mute stones speak, even when they can find them, without a thorough knowledge of the literature. And about Tartessus there is a great deal of literary evidence. For example, the Romans regularly confused the lost Tartessus with Cádiz; it may be to Tartessus that the Roman historian Velleius Paterculus is referring when he dates the foundation of Cádiz 80 years after the Trojan War, which he thought ended at a date corresponding to 1184 B.C.

Then there is myth, which to the archaeologist is prehistory. The ancient name of Lisbon was Olisipo, which the ancients derived from Ulysses. The golden apples of the Hesperides grew in Spain, and it was one of Heracles's labors to gather them. Another labor involved rustling the cattle of the triple-bodied Geryon. In myth he is one

---

* See *The Mute Stones Speak*, p. 58, Fig. 2.20.

of the kings of Tartessus, and his triple body might symbolize the three mouths of the Guadalquivir. The cattle of Andalucia—the modern name for the kingdom of Tartessus—are still the most prized in Spain; it is 1,000-pound Andalucian bulls that fight in the Spanish arenas. Plato's description of the lost city of Atlantis, near the Pillars of Hercules, with its triple walls coated with bronze, tin, and orichalcum, might reflect the metals that made Tartessus rich; and it was Atlas, king of Atlantis, who got the golden apples for Heracles. The wealth in precious metals of the magic palace of Alcinous in the *Odyssey* might have come from Tartessus, and Homer's description might be a reflection of Phocaean sailors' yarns of what they had seen in the golden west.

Myth provides only material for inference. When archaeologists pass from myth to literature, they find the earliest reference to Tartessus in Stesichorus, of Himera in Sicily, who, about the end of the seventh century B.C., mentions "the boundless silver-rooted springs of Tartessus River." Fifty years later the lyric poet Anacreon of Teos wrote, "I shouldn't want to live for 150 years like the King of Tartessus." Now Teos, where Anacreon came from, is only 36 miles from Phocaea, which colonized the far west, and the king that Anacreon refers to is the fabulous Arganthonius, who reigned for 80 years and gave the Phocaeans money to build their city wall against the Persians. Herodotus knows all about him—though he thinks he lived to be only 120—and records his friendship with the Phocaeans, which would place his reign about 630–550 B.C. Now early in that reign—again according to Herodotus—the adventurer Colaeus of Samos—36 miles from Teos, 72 from Phocaea—was blown by a strong wind beyond the Pillars of Hercules to Tartessus, and brought back the second richest cargo of his time: out of the tithe due to Hera the Samians made a bronze mixing bowl with griffins' heads, supported by three bronze giants seven cubits tall; Colaeus's share of the profit was 54 talents, which works out to $64,800 uninflated.

It would appear that Tartessus grew rich on its mines, its industry, and its overseas trade; its very troughs and barrels, and its anchors, according to Greek travelers' tales, were of silver. But its culture matched its wealth, as we can tell not only from the tastefulness of the gold work in the Villena and El Carambolo treasures, but also from the fact that it had annals, epics, and laws in verse, as in the ancient Near East. These do not survive, but we are told that they were written in an as yet undeciphered language, which in historical times the Tartessians wrote in a Greek alphabet. In 1940 in south Portugal, well within the boundaries of the ancient Tartessian kingdom, was found an inscription in this alphabet which closely resembles one from Lemnos in Asia Minor.* Now Lemnos is near where the Etruscans may have come from; the name of Tartessus looks rather like "Tyrseni," which is what Herodotus calls the Etruscans; and the "orientalizing" gold pectoral in the El Carambolo treasure looks, as we saw, like one from Etruscan Caere. So Schulten thought that Tartessus was founded by the ancestors of the Etruscans. Later scholars are not so sure, but all are agreed that Tartessian culture owed much to the Near East. If we suppose the original settlers of Tartessus to have been invaders like the Etruscans, then Tartessian culture in its classical phase was an amalgam of these invaders with the aborigines. This amalgam the world was later to call Iberian, and the later Iberian alphabet is an adaptation of the one on the inscription from south Portugal. Modern Andalucians are very proud of this long and storied background.

Jonah's ship to Tarshish sailed from Jaffa—now part of Tel Aviv— in ancient times often in Phoenician hands. King Hiram of Phoenician Tyre had, according to the Bible, fleets that plied the seas with the fleets of Tarshish, and Tyre founded Cádiz, which grew to be Tartessus's rival. No remains at Cádiz are dated earlier than the eighth century B.C., but from this time on the Phoenicians, as we shall see, founded trading posts systematically along the south coast of Spain, and Tartessus must have felt the rivalry keenly. Carthage was a Tyrian settlement, too, and the advent of the Carthaginians in Spain boded no good for Tartessus.

With the Phoenicians there was rivalry; with the Greeks there was friendship. The Greeks, like the Phoenicians, came to the Iberian peninsula after metal. (The Greek words for "gold" and "copper" are borrowed from Phoenician.) The treasury of Sicyon at Olympia contained Tartessian bronze; "Corinthian" helmets of the seventh and sixth centuries B.C., perhaps made in Spain, have been found at the mouth of the Guadalete (in Greek, "Menestheus' Harbor") and at Huelva (Fig. 2.4). From the Greek colonies in Spain—of which

---

* See *The Mute Stones Speak*, p. 27, Fig. 2.1.

more later—came Greek influence upon Tartessus. But in 535 B.C. the Phocaeans lost so many ships off Corsica in the naval battle of Alalia against the Carthaginians that the range of their trade in the West contracted. The Carthaginians soon closed the Straits of Gibraltar and destroyed Tartessus utterly, sometime between 520 and 505 B.C. Henceforward Carthage paid her soldiers with Tartessian silver, and the Greek Pindar wrote, "Beyond the Pillars of Hercules no wise man can tread; no fool either." So fell an old and cultured people, a prosperous empire of hospitable men of peace. The Romans were to sneer at the descendants of the Tartessians for being "extremely unwarlike"; they hired mercenaries to do their fighting for them. But in that civilized culture, with its aversion to war, the arts flourished. Such masterpieces of later Spanish art as the Dama de Elche owe something to Tartessus, and if the Romans found the Romanization of south Spain easy, they had the civilized mildness of the posterity of Arganthonius to thank for it.

FIGURE 2.4
Huelva, bronze
Corinthian
helmet

We turn next to the archaeological evidence for Punic—that is, Phoenician-Carthaginian—Spain. The Phoenicians were a hard-headed, businesslike people. Their interest in art was minimal, their art forms derivative. Hence, archaeological remains which can be clearly identified as Punic are sparse.

The most important Punic city in Spain was Cádiz (Punic Gadir: the fortress). The name at once strikes a bellicose note: the city was founded on an impregnable island, its citizens were intrepid sailors, and it was in Cádiz that the battering-ram was invented. Its lighthouse, 120 cubits high with a gilt bronze statue eight cubits high on top, survived until it fell, undermined by treasure seekers, about A.D. 1000. Its superior port installations made it the natural port of departure for Hanno, the Cathaginian sailor who explored the West African coast before 480 B.C. If it was really founded in the late twelfth century B.C., as Velleius says, it is the oldest city in the West. If we are to set its foundation date more cautiously—in the eighth century, on the archaeological evidence—it is still of very respectable antiquity, as old as Rome. Its most important temple was to Moloch, god of fire, to whom children were sacrificed; the Greeks identified him with Cronus (the Roman Saturn) who ate his offspring. There is irony in the fact that the Cádiz cathedral now stands on the spot where this cannibal god was worshiped.

Cádiz became a melting pot: in its teeming streets Tartessians and Greeks rubbed elbows with Phoenicians. The Greeks identified the Phoenician city god Melkart with Heracles; Melkart-Heracles had at the base of the island, 12 miles from the city (a mile for each labor), a seaside temple, now submerged (fishermen still occasionally drag up finds from it in their nets). Women and pigs were barred from its precincts; the barefoot, shaven-headed, silent priests, dressed in white robes bordered with purple, tended an eternal flame. It had roof beams which never needed replacing (cedar of Lebanon?), the labors of Heracles were engraved on the doors. On two bronze columns before the temple, the temple accounts were engraved on tablets of precious metal in a language illegible to our Greek source—probably in a Semitic alphabet. Some scholars see in the pair of bronze columns the factual origin of the myth of the Pillars of Hercules (for the land masses at the narrowest point of the Straits of Gibraltar, between Tarifa and Benzú, are not pillar-like at all).

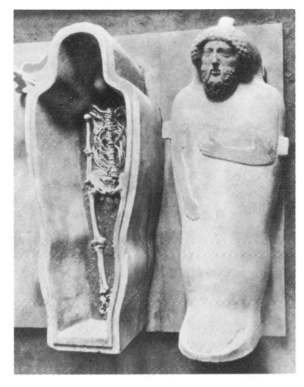

FIGURE 2.5

Cádiz, Museo Arqueológico Provincial, anthropoid sarcophagus with cover removed

Just outside the gate of the city was the Punic necropolis where, since 1878, 150 rich tombs have been excavated, unfortunately without scientific archaeological supervision, so that the finds can only be dated vaguely between the fifth and the second centuries B.C. The most famous find is the anthropoid sarcophagus (Fig. 2.5) now in the Cádiz museum. It is of marble and was originally cedar-lined; the features show Greek influence. Interesting also is the head of a Negro, in terracotta (Fig. 2.6).

Cádiz had a reputation, especially in Roman times, as a rich and wicked city. It had tall houses (it is still the only city in Andalucia with houses of more than three stories) with widow's walks on top, from which the women could watch for the return of their husbands from adventurous voyages to strange lands. Cádiz in Roman times had 500 millionaires—more than any other city in the Roman world except Rome and Padua. The wealth came from the export of metals, grain, oil, wine, wax, honey, pitch (for caulking ships), cochineal (red dye), and tiles, all exported in huge freighters. Cádiz was notorious for its provocative dancers. They used castanets, as the Andalucian flamenco dancers do today. They were much in demand at Roman parties; a friend of Pliny's cut a gourmet dinner because he heard there were to be *puellae Gaditanae*—and oysters—at another party. The girls' gyrations (bumps and grinds?) would tempt a Hippolytus. Eudoxus, the Greek sailor who explored the West African coast, took some dancing girls with him to dazzle the chiefs; then never came back. Managers exploited the girls shamefully, enslaving them and forcing them (with how pretty a show of reluctance?) to go on tour.

Until recently, very few Punic sites in Spain had been scientifically excavated. But in 1962 in digging the foundations for some government flats at Almuñécar (Granada) on the south coast, the builders hit upon 20 rock-cut tombs which turned out to be Punic, and

FIGURE 2.6
Cádiz, Museo Arqueológico Provincial, terracotta head of a Negro from Isla de León necropolis, profile and full-face

FIGURE 2.7
*Madrid, Museo
Arqueológico Nacional,
painted ostrich egg from
Punic cemetery at Vil-
laricos, used as a cos
metics container*

Old Punic at that; an inscription in Old Punic (the language as used
in the Old Country, Phoenicia, before the sixth century B.C.); alabaster jars, imported from Egypt long before the burials, bearing in
the oval rings called cartouches the names, in hieroglyphs, of pharaohs
of the ninth century B.C.; gold, silver, and copper rings; bronze
bracelets; and (a specialty of Punic graves) a decorated ostrich egg,
filled with red ocher and used as a container for cosmetics. (Fig. 2.7.
The one illustrated is not from Almuñécar but from the site excavated
by the Sirets at Villaricos, up the coast toward Cartagena; there is a
large and typical collection on the second floor of the Museo Arqueológico Nacional in Madrid.) But what interested Pellicer, the excavator, most of all was a vase which was not Punic at all, but Greek:
a flat-bottomed bowl with handles level with the rim, called a
kotyle. What excited Pellicer was the fact that the vase was of the
type called Proto-Corinthian; it could only have been made between
700 and 675 B.C. This means that the cemetery at Almuñécar is
the first really ancient Punic necropolis yet dated in Spain. The ones
already known in Cádiz, at Villaricos, at Puig d'es Molins on the
island of Ibiza in the Balearics, and at Tosal de Manises (Alicante)
are all sixth century or later. The grave contents come exclusively
from the Near East; these are the burials of the settlers of Punic Sexi,

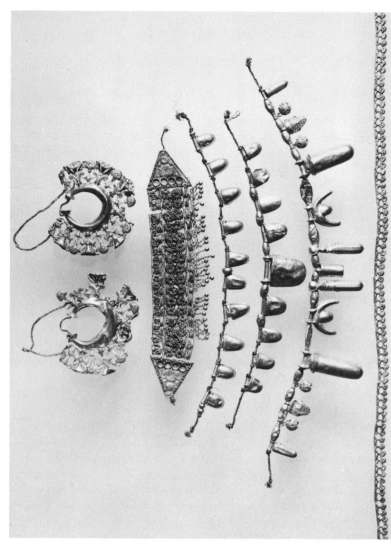

FIGURE 2.8
Madrid, Museo Arqueológico Nacional, gold earrings, diadem, necklaces, and chain from La Aliseda treasure

and they are the mortal remains of some of the first Near-Easterners to set foot in Spain.

In 1964 Pellicer joined with H. G. Niemeyer and H. Schubart of the German Archaeological Institute in Madrid to dig seven trial trenches near Torre del Mar (Málaga) at the mouth of the Rio Vélez 18 miles east of Málaga. Schulten, who had excavated here in 1922, believed this to be the site of the Greek colony of Mainake, but the new dig did not confirm his view. The level immediately below the Arab phase of the ninth to the twelfth centuries A.D. proved to be Punic. Again, it was a Greek vase that provided the first clue to the dating: a very rare sherd of a Greek amphora of the seventh century B.C. Later, carbon 14 analysis of appropriate materials gave the date 670 B.C. ± 140 years. Since then further exploration has enabled Pellicer and his colleagues to announce the discovery of a total of four certain Punic factories on the south coast, all near the mouths of the Rios Vélez and Algarrobo.

The most spectacular Punic find to date in Spain was turned up in 1920 by workmen digging the foundations for a brick works at La Aliseda (Cáceres). It is a gold treasure whose workmanship enables it to be dated in the sixth century B.C.: exquisite filigree earrings, a diadem with filigree rosettes set with turquoise, necklaces exactly like those worn by the Dama de Elche (one of them with falcons among the charms), a chain (Fig. 2.8), a heavy bracelet in very fine granulated work (Fig. 2.9), and (not illustrated) a golden girdle, an amethyst scarab, rings in appliqué, a bronze mirror, some glass, and a Carthaginian silver pitcher. Though the fabulous keepsakes are themselves of the sixth century B.C., the treasure was not buried until the collapse of the Carthaginian Spanish Empire before the Romans in the third. Before an archaeologist could arrive, the precious objects were sold in Cáceres, but the government intervened, and they are now on display in the Museo Arqueológico, Madrid.

After Nebuchadnezzar destroyed Tyre in 573 B.C., Carthage replaced her as mistress of the Mediterranean. The Carthaginians were early tempted by the fertile soil, the pleasant climate, and the military and commercial possibilities of the Balearic Islands. Mahon, the chief town of Menorca, probably takes its name from Mago, who founded Carthaginian military power about 520 B.C.

The largest Punic necropolis ever excavated—4,000 burials, arranged staircase-fashion up the side of a hill—was found in 1910 at

FIGURE 2.9
*Madrid, Museo Ar-
queológico Nacional,
heavy gold bracelet
with granulation,
from La Aliseda
treasure*

Puig d'es Molins (Mill Hill in Catalan) on the island of Ibiza; a selection of the finds is to be seen in the Museo Arqueológico Provincial, Barcelona, and in the Museo Arqueológico Nacional, Madrid. The tombs had been pretty thoroughly pillaged long before 1910: A. Vives, the excavator, found on the floors lamps left by grave robbers from Moorish times, who tunneled from tomb to tomb. The burials date from about 500 B.C. to Roman times. Besides pins, bracelets, coins, rings, silver and bronze mirrors, keys, scissors, necklaces, spoons, fishhooks, pottery, clay seals, molds, lamps, bronze cymbals and bells, bone flutes, amulets, votive axes, and the ubiquitous painted ostrich eggs, all of which are interesting but common enough, there were some finds of unusual importance or oddity: grotesque death masks like those used to ward off evil spirits in the Temple of Artemis Orthia in Sparta; * crude, mass-produced phallic figurines, humpty-dumpty shaped, holding their testicles in one hand and a lamp on their heads (there is still a large clandestine trade in these). There is a crude attempt at imitating Greek art in the terra cotta busts of goddesses

---

* See *The Greek Stones Speak*, p. 149, Fig. 3.16.

(perhaps likenesses of Tanit, the virgin moon deity) made from molds and heavily bejeweled, with their curiously stick-like arms grotesquely out of anatomical proportion, inserted separately and held within by dowels (Fig. 2.10). The Catalan visitors to the Barcelona museum are delighted with the narrow-spouted drinking vessels designed to be used with the spout held at some distance from the mouth—they use them every day themselves, and call them *porrones*.

A pair of isolated finds must complete our survey of Punic Spain.

FIGURE 2.10

Barcelona, Museo Arqueológico Provincial, terra cotta statuette, probably of Punic goddess Tanit, from Puig d'es Molins (Ibiza) necropolis

FIGURE 2.11
Madrid, Museo Arqueológico Nacional, bronze head of bull from Costix (*Mallorca*)

From Costix on Mallorca comes (Fig. 2.11) the massive, splendidly fierce bronze bull's head (it weighs 72.6 pounds) to remind us how old and perhaps how foreign is the bull cult which brings death in the afternoon to these splendid beasts in Spain; and from Galera

FIGURE 2.12
*Madrid, Museo
Arqueológico
Nacional, ala-
baster statuette
of Punic god-
dess, perhaps
Astarte, from
Galera (Gra-
nada)*

(Granada) comes the little alabaster goddess (Fig. 2.12), perhaps
Astarte, goddess of love, only eight inches high, flanked by sphinxes,
her breasts pierced so that milk poured in through her head may
flow from them into the bowl she holds in her lap.

The total effect of the archaeological evidence for Tartessian and
Punic culture in Spain must be to underline the enormous wealth

in precious metals of the peninsula—and this is up to a point right, for it was metals that attracted all the exploiters: the Tartessians and Phoenicians themselves, Carthaginians, Greeks, and Romans, each of whom made their impact upon the indigenous Iberian culture. But it would be a mistake to judge from the cultural and historical importance of gold treasures like those of Villena, El Carambolo, or La Aliseda that the aim of Spanish archaeology is treasure hunting. For too long, it is true, in Spain as well as in other countries, the aim of excavation was to find *objets d'art* for private collections and museums. But modern scientific archaeologists are interested in gold not so much for its intrinsic value—though it is only human to be pleased when you find nine kilos of beautiful jewelry in a pot—but for what it can tell about the cultural history of the people who lived in Spain from 1100 to 500 B.C. And for this, as we have seen, a datable potsherd or a Proto-Corinthian vase can be as important as a gold diadem.

3

THE GREEKS IN SPAIN: EMPORION

(600 B.C.–A.D. 300)

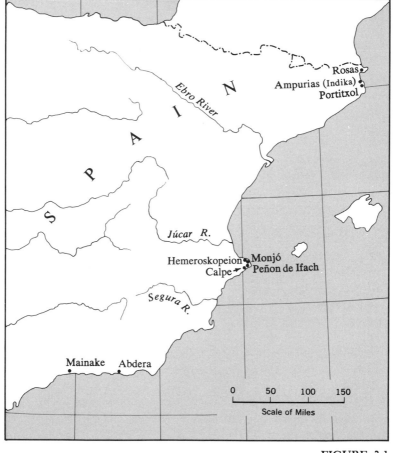

FIGURE 3.1
The Greeks in Spain

Since 1962 THE SPANISH ARCHAEOLOGIST MI-
guel Oliva has been excavating at Rosas (Gerona), ancient Rhode, a
Rhodian foundation on the Costa Brava (see map, Fig. 3.1) dated in
legend before 776 B.C., though the oldest datable objects he found
are not earlier than the sixth century. This land in the far west, 1,500
miles from home, must have seemed congenial to the Greek colonists,
for the climate and the landscape were strikingly like what they were
used to: hot summers, mild winters, lending themselves to the cultiva-
tion of the indispensable vine and olive; the vivid blue of sea and sky,
bright colors, steep cliffs, sandy beaches, and everywhere the heady but
familiar odor of thyme and mint. Oliva excavated at the Ciudadela,
just north of the modern highway at the entrance to the town. He
found, under the church of the eleventh century A.D., Ionian and
Phocaean pottery of the sixth century, Attic ware of the fifth, and a
whole sequence, following this, of Apulian and Campanian ware, at-
testing to the occupation of the site down into Roman times; a Hellenistic grid of streets and houses; Greek, Punic, and Roman coins.

There were Greek colonies in Spain, imperfectly known and inade-
quately excavated, at Hemeroskopeion (Denia [Alicante]), Akra Leuke
(Tosal de Manises [Alicante]), Abdera (Adra [Almería]), and Mainake
(east of Málaga). Of these Hemeroskopeion ("Day-Watch") has received the most attention in modern times. Its modern name, Denia,
is a corruption of Latin Diana, the Greek Artemis, who was worshiped here as at Palaiopolis (see below); Cean-Bermudez, writing in
1832, remarks that antiquities from the temple are the playthings of
the children of the town, in their "barbarism and ignorance." The
watch may have been kept from nearby Monjó, 2,437 feet high, though
Rhys Carpenter would locate the Greek colony near Calpe, a dozen

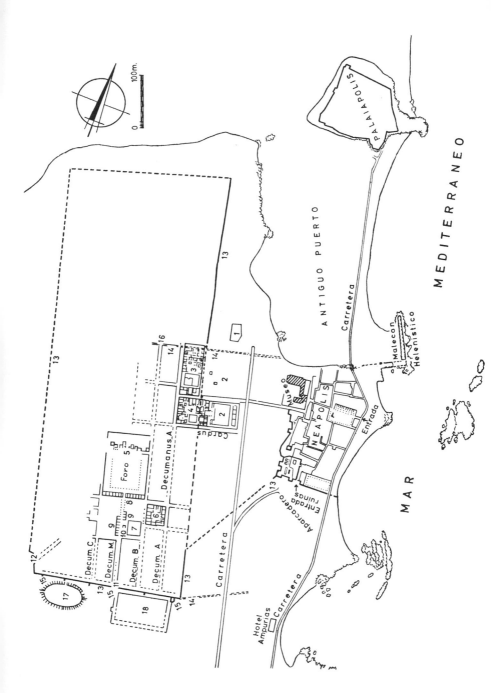

miles to the south, where he found Greek pottery on the spectacular, Gibraltar-like Peñon de Ifach, which would also have made a good watchtower.

But by far the most important and best-excavated Greek site in Spain is Ampurias (Gerona), Greek Emporion, "the Market," at the south end of the Gulf of Rosas. The site has been known and studied since 1775, but scientific excavation there did not begin until this century '(1908); dating by pottery types began in 1939 and by stratigraphy in 1959. Emporion was founded from Massilia (Marseilles), and Massilia from Phocaea. The oldest settlement, Palaiopolis, lies under the present hamlet of San Martín de Ampurias (Fig. 3.2). The site, now a promontory, was in ancient times an island. Its great antiquity was first noticed in 1912, when workmen digging the foundations for a summer place came upon blocks of a Greek wall, which were broken up and removed. The owner kept a sculptured fragment—a pair of sphinxes back-to-back—as a decoration for his dining room. As time passed, the Costa Brava became more and more popular as a summer resort, property values increased, and the proprietor of the land where the Greek blocks were found was most reluctant to sell. But he was finally persuaded, and excavation began within and adjoining a circular tower of the tenth century A.D. Nine levels were distinguished. The lowest, containing Ionic and Phocaean, Attic and Corinthian pottery, together with local gray ware and the shiny black Etruscan glaze called

FIGURE 3.2
Ampurias, plan, showing Palaiopolis, Neapolis, and Roman town

1. Late Roman cemetery	7. Public building	Julius Caesar
2. Gardens of Roman houses	8. Double colonnade crossing commercial forum	14. Wall of native settlement of Indika
3. Roman house I		15. Remains of towers, Indika wall
4. Roman house II	9. Shops	
5. Temples and public buildings facing Roman forum	10. Temple	16. North gate, Indika wall
	11. South gate of Roman wall	17. Amphitheater (Claudian)
	12. Southeast gate of Roman wall	18. Palaestra (Claudian)
6. Block southeast of commercial forum	13. Roman wall of the time of	

bucchero, was dated in the sixth century B.C. This is where the colonists
of Ampurias lived until 575 B.C. when they transferred to a new site,
Neapolis, across the now silted harbor to the south. The eighth level
of Palaiopolis proved to contain Iberian and Campanian ware, dated
down into the second century B.C., proof that the site continued to be
inhabited after the majority of the population moved. The seventh
level was that of the Hellenistic wall discovered in 1912; seven courses
of fine squared sandstone blocks were still standing. The higher levels
were Visigothic and mediaeval. The geographer Strabo reports a temple of the many-breasted Ephesian Artemis in Palaiopolis: it probably
lies under the present church of San Martín.

Not long after the move from the old city to the new, in 540 B.C.,
King Cyrus of Persia destroyed the original mother-city, Phocaea, and
Emporion lost a link with the old Greece. After the battle of Alalia, in
535 B.C., Carthaginian influence grew in the western Mediterranean.
To meet it, the town fortifications were strengthened. The present
town wall is of the type called Cyclopean, built of huge unsquared
stones fitted together without mortar. Such walls used to be believed
to be of remote antiquity, but more recent studies tend to down-date
them. Professor Martín Almagro, the excavator of Emporion, thinks its
wall, which measures 650 by 407 feet, was a strengthening of the
original wall in 237 B.C. against the Carthaginian general Hamilcar,
Hannibal's father.

The sole entrance to Neapolis was by a gate in the south wall, at the
extreme left center of the air photograph (Fig. 3.3); the town fathers
in rotation kept constant guard there. In the upper left corner of the
excavated area the largest rectangular building is the Temple of
Asclepius, god of health (Fig. 3.4); the statue of the god, larger than
life, set up on the spot, is a cement copy; the original, of Pentelic
marble, is in the Museo Arqueológico in Barcelona, the only large
scale Greek statue yet discovered in Spain. It has been ascribed to
Phidias (mid-fifth century B.C.), but Almagro thinks it is Hellenistic,
of about 225 B.C. The building to the southeast of it is an open-air
shrine adapted for religious or secular meetings, identified by Almagro
as a *sacellum* or *bouleuterion* (Council House). To the north of the
Asclepius temple, across an unexcavated area, is a tower from which
the citizens, divided into three watches, kept a constant lookout. Under
the unexcavated fields at the top of the photograph lay the native
town, called Indika; traces of its wall, towers, and gate are indicated
on the plan, Fig. 3.2: 14, 15, 16. The town wall of Neapolis formed

an Iron Curtain between the Greeks and the Iberian population, and
no love was lost between them. Patriotic modern Spaniards infer from
the evidence that the Greeks were a mere outnumbered enclave, and
that the Iberians preserved their independence. There is some cor-
roboration of this view in the idiosyncrasy of the Iberian vase (Fig.
4.20) showing hunters with lances pursuing a stag, now in the Barcelona museum.

The oval below the watchtower is a Hellenistic cistern, in which
rain water was filtered through amphoras filled with charcoal and sand
(Fig. 3.5).

FIGURE 3.3

*Ampurias, air view of early phase of excavations. Lower left, precinct of
Serapis. Modern building, upper right, is the site museum*

FIGURE 3.4

Ampurias, precinct of Asclepius, model

The open precinct (90 by 130 feet) in the lower left corner of the air photograph is the Temple of Zeus Serapis, an Egyptian deity, identified from a bilingual inscription, in Greek and Latin—one of a series, in these languages and in Iberian, which the soil of Emporion has yielded. The building closely resembles the Temple of Isis at Pompeii and is of Roman date, perhaps 100 B.C. The Egyptian warship, popular with sailors, reminds us that Emporion was a port town, with cosmopolitan connections. Figure 3.6 shows the model of the temple in the Barcelona museum. The temple stands on a high podium, Roman fashion, and is surrounded by a shady colonnade.

The air photograph is an old one. The extent of excavation since it was taken is revealed by comparison between it and the model (Fig. 3.7), also in the Barcelona museum. The model shows, starting from

FIGURE 3.5

Ampurias, amphoras used in water filtration

FIGURE 3.6
Ampurias, temple and precinct of Serapis, model in Museo Arqueológico Provincial, Barcelona

the northwest corner of the temple precinct, the wide main street of Emporion, leading to the wide open space (right center) of the agorá, "where the Greeks meet to cheat each other," as Herodotus reports a cynical Persian as saying. It, too, was surrounded by a portico, in typical Hellenistic fashion; Almagro compares it, on a small scale, with the Hellenistic Asia Minor town of Priene.* The three foundations at the back are those of the town offices, as in the Forum at Pompeii. The 45-foot-wide street leading eastward from the agorá to the sea was also pleasantly colonnaded.

The blocks of houses which fill the rest of the model are of Hellenistic and Roman date, and on the whole modest or poor. The best houses were near the sea; one with a peristyle or patio is visible in the lower right corner of the model; another, paved with waterproof cement, has a meander pattern inset in white pebbles and an inscription, in Greek, "Hail, Good Spirit." In one of the houses, in 1926, was found a hoard of 894 coins.

The buildings at the back of the model are those of a monastery, renovated into a museum and workrooms. Most of the major finds from

---

* See *The Greek Stones Speak,* pp. 309–312, Fig. 6.15.

Emporion are in the Barcelona museum, and are of Roman date; for example, the mosaic of Agamemnon about to sacrifice Iphigenia (Fig. 3.8). He holds her by the wrist before the altar. Artemis, who both demanded the sacrifice and saved the victim, appears twice: once, with Apollo, as a statue surmounting a column; again (upper right) holding by an antler the stag she substituted for Iphigenia at the last moment. Another is the splendid realistic portrait head of a lady (Fig. 3.9), found in the Roman town to the west (Fig. 3.2), in the house of which she was mistress. Art historians date sculpture by the hairdo: hers was in fashion about 25 B.C. Still another is a bronze lamp from Alexandria, inlaid with silver and gold, and worked into the shape of a head with strongly Semitic features. And enough of a catapult was found to make it possible to reconstruct it. It will fire with accuracy up to 100 yards; tension was provided by twisted hair—that of either a woman or a horse would do. There are swords, arrowheads, and sling bullets to remind us that Greek Emporion did not yield to the Romans without a struggle. A trident for spearing fish gives mute evidence of a peace-time occupation, and a jointed terracotta doll of the presence, too often forgotten, of children playing in a live city.

FIGURE 3.7
Ampurias, Neapolis, model, Museo Arqueológico Provincial, Barcelona

But even a live city must bury its dead. The necropolis of Greek Emporion lies some 500 yards south of the town, at Portitxol. The graves are lined with tiles whose stamps, in Greek, show that they came from a public tile factory. The cemetery yielded quantities of proto-Corinthian, Corinthian, and Rhodian ware from the sixth century onward; the Greek vases from Emporion are a distinguished collection; Sir John Beazley has named one of the artists "the Ampurias painter." On the vases women play the lyre and flute; there are satyrs

FIGURE 3.8

Barcelona, Museo Arqueológico Provincial, mosaic of sacrifice of Iphigenia, from Ampurias

FIGURE 3.9
Barcelona, Museo Arqueológico Provincial, portrait bust of Roman matron, from Ampurias

and Bacchantes, Greeks and Amazons, Lapiths and Centaurs. There is a bronze panther head, perhaps Etruscan, of about 550 B.C., which perhaps once decorated the end of a chariot pole; a tortoise in blue glass paste; and numerous coins. Emporion had its own mint until the time of Julius Caesar, with the nymph Arethusa on the obverse and the winged horse Pegasus on the reverse. Since Arethusa is a Syracusan type, and Pegasus a Corinthian, the coins help to make Emporion's trading connections clear; and there are others from south Italy (Thurii, Velia), Asia Minor (Phocaea, Miletus, Teos, Chios, Rhodes), and the faraway Crimea. Only one Athenian coin was found: Emporion's imports from Attica (the pottery) apparently exceeded her exports to it. Coins from Emporion have turned up from as far away as Westphalia, Guimarães in Portugal, and Seville.

The Greeks of Emporion were interested in trade, and therefore in peace, and in any imperialist power that seemed likely to preserve it. As long as the Carthaginian Empire in Spain was expanding, especially between 237 and 219 B.C., the Greeks, secure behind their wall, did business with it. But Rome was another expanding empire, and Rome developed interests in Spain. When Hannibal invaded Italy, in 218 B.C., it was in Rome's interest to prevent reinforcements from reaching him. Rome had a treaty of friendship with Massilia, and Emporion had ties of blood, sentiment, and commerce with Rome. So when Gnaeus Scipio, uncle of the great Africanus, arrived off the port with a fleet in 218 B.C., the Greeks let him land. His victories both military and diplomatic gained Rome much profit. He sent 14,342 pounds of silver back to the treasury. Rome also gained local adherents, and Roman influence in northeast Spain began to be established, though there were to be nearly 200 years of stubborn, sanguinary resistance before Spain finally acquiesced in her status as a Roman province.

But when Cato, Roman consul in 195 B.C., after the defeat of Carthage in the Second Punic War, was assigned to Spain—to which the Carthaginian defeat had established a claim by default—Scipio's landing had established a precedent. Cato disembarked his troops at Emporion, too, used the port as a training base, pacified the back-country by force, and exploited the mines. He shipped back to Rome 25,000 pounds of silver and 1,400 of gold. In their first 50 years in Spain, the Romans sent home 1,754,510 uninflated dollars' worth of precious metals, a yearly average of five per cent of the entire state income. To the Roman ruling class, such riches were worth any amount of bloodshed; the lure of the Spanish mines goes far to explain Rome's bleeding herself white in Spain for the next five generations. Many a general famous in Roman history served in Spain: Tiberius Gracchus, father of two tribunes; Scipio the Younger, adoptive grandson of Africanus; Pompey the Great; Julius Caesar; Augustus' lieutenant Agrippa; and Augustus himself.

Of these it is to Julius Caesar that Roman Emporion owed its founding. Since the area had been pro-Pompeian in the Civil War of 49–45 B.C., Emporion seemed a strategic place to settle time-expired veterans, who could be counted on to keep a watchful eye on anti-Caesarian activities in the district. This is the most convenient place to discuss Roman Emporion. It is not entirely irrelevant to a consideration of the Greeks in Spain, since it is an example of Greek culture under Roman impact; tombstones show that Greek men married Roman women; the Greek language survived; and Greek art adorned Roman houses.

Roman Emporiae (the Latin spelling) was planned on a huge scale, behind a vast rectangular wall, 150 yards west of the Greek town; its area, 975 by 2,275 feet, was some ten times that of Neapolis. On the south, the wall still stands 16 feet high, built of roughly-squared blocks in the lower courses, concrete above (Fig. 3.10); at its base the excavators found the remains of fallen battlements; some of its towers, as we saw, formerly served the Iberian town of Indika.

Outside the wall, and protected by it from the north wind, are the amphitheater (Fig. 3.11) and the palaestra. The amphitheater had wooden seats—the excavators found the nails—and so was a fire hazard, an additional reason for locating it outside the wall. It was built in the reign of Claudius (A.D. 41–54) and is 312 feet long, standard for a modest provincial arena, but only about half the size of the Coliseum in Rome. Amphitheaters, in which gladiators fought

FIGURE 3.10

Ampurias, wall and gate of Roman town

FIGURE 3.11
Ampurias, remains of Roman amphitheater

to the death, satisfied the cultural needs of the sons of Italy; the palaestra (Fig. 3.2, 18) was a wrestling ground, designed for Greek tastes. Under its portico, athletes could practice foot racing in the shade; once up and down its long side was a stade (600 feet), the standard length for Greek running races.

The central gate in the south wall opened into a porticoed main street, the *cardo maximus* (mislabeled *decumanus* on Almagro's plan); it led north, past rows of shops and a temple (perhaps of Rome and Augustus) to the porticoed forum—corresponding to the agorá in Neapolis—with more shops on its south side and public buildings on the north. Its central space is paved with sandstone. Southeast of it (6 on the plan) an entire city block was devoted to more shops; the building at 7 may have been the basilica, which doubled as law court and indoor market for use in rainy weather. The rest of the southern half of the town has not been excavated.

The Italian scholar Nino Lamboglia made in 1959 a careful stratigraphic study in the street by Roman House I (3 on the plan). This is not far from a gate (16 on the plan) of Iberian Indika, over which

Roman Emporiae was built, so the lowest of his seven levels contained Iberian pottery; he dated it 350–190 B.C. The sixth level contained Campanian ware, imported from Italy, dated 190–100 B.C. Then there was a blank, indicating the abandonment, perhaps the destruction, of the Iberian settlement, and when the pottery starts again it is the rosy embossed Arretine ware, or *terra sigillata* (Level v, 30 B.C. to A.D. 40). The top three levels take the history of the Roman town down to A.D. 300, when it perished at the hands of the barbarians.

Northeast of the forum (2, 3, 4 on the plan) are two elegant late-Republican Roman houses with gardens and mosaics. The gardens have been replanted (with trellises, cypresses, laurels, and potted aromatic plants) and the mosaics restored (Fig. 3.12) to give the visitor a vivid and colorful idea of what Roman Emporiae was like in its prime. One house (3 on the plan) had baths, built-in benches, painted stucco walls, and a children's play enclosure. The mosaic motifs include a Greek actor's mask and a partridge pecking at a basket of

FIGURE 3.12

Ampurias, Roman town, geometric mosaic in situ

worms. Part of the city wall was taken down to give the owners a better sea view; that military needs might be sacrificed to aesthetics is one of the meanings of the *pax Romana*. But, just to be on the safe side, the wall was extended farther south (13 on the plan) to connect with the Greek wall of Neapolis; it was such precautions as this that kept the Roman peace in being. In the women's quarters of this house was found the strong-faced portrait head of the proprietress, illustrated in Figure 3.9. The building of the other house (4 on the plan) also necessitated dismantling a section of the town wall. Though the house is of Roman date (50–25 B.C.) it is a veritable Hellenistic palace in the Greek fashion; it has no less than three peristyles or patios, one with two fountains and two pieces of Greek statuary (herms). Another has its retaining walls stuccoed, painted black, and decorated with painted columns in red. The altar in this peristyle was stuccoed and painted with a cock and two snakes drinking from a wine bowl. The third peristyle has a comfortably curved Greek garden seat, or exedra. The two rooms flanking the atrium are richly painted; there is a handsome mosaic with a pattern of black and white stars; and, like its neighbor, it has its own private baths.

A comparison between Roman Emporiae and Greek Neapolis is illuminating. The public parts of the Roman town are more orderly in arrangement, the private parts more sumptuous. The amphitheater is a concession to Roman taste. But in Roman Emporiae, as elsewhere in the Roman world, it is evident that captive Greece took captive her fierce conqueror, and brought Greek sophistication where there might have been only Roman rusticity. The porticoes, the palaestra, the peristyles, and most of the statuary, mosaics, and pottery are Greek in inspiration; in this little town at the world's end was kept up, with Rome as intermediary, the age-old culture of the Near East from which Emporion ultimately sprang. But between the Greek and the Roman town lay the Iberian settlement, and it is to the Iberians that we next turn.

4

THE
IBERIAN
RESIS-
TANCE

(ca. 600 B.C.-A.D. 337)

T HIS BOOK IS CALLED *THE IBERIAN STONES Speak* in order to embrace within one short title both Spain and Portugal, which in antiquity were one. But this is a purely geographical usage, and may cause confusion unless I emphasize here that archaeologists use "Iberian" also to designate a brave, highly talented, and original native people whose towns and artifacts, found in the Spanish Levant, Catalonia, and the Ebro Valley, date from the sixth century B.C. until well down into Roman times. A combination of literary and archaeological evidence reveals the Iberians as a suffering, stoical, frugal, quarrelsome people, devoted to bulls and horses, simple in diversions, suspicious of strangers and neighbors, religious to the point of superstition, respecting their elders. So far as it is possible to generalize about any people, what I have just written might as well be a thumbnail sketch of the Spaniard of today. They are also surprisingly like the Etruscans.* They forged an idiosyncratic culture; they were doomed to fall before the Romans; they spoke and wrote an as yet undeciphered language; they were superstitious; and, as free interpreters of classicism, they were culturally a Third Force, between East and West.

Iberians liked to live in hilltop towns, of which one of the oldest and best excavated is Ullastret, 20 miles east of Gerona and 9 miles

---

* See *The Mute Stones Speak*, Chap. 2.

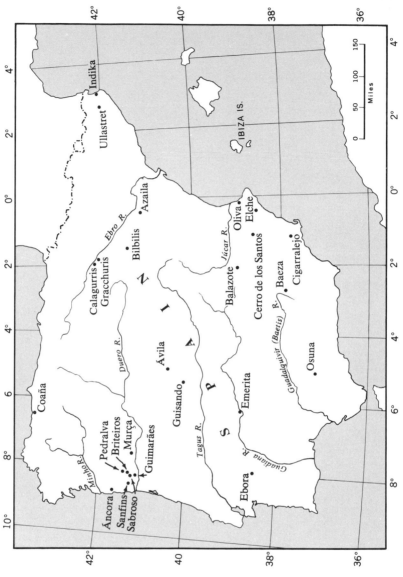

FIGURE 4.1
Iberian and
Celtic sites in
Spain and
Portugal

FIGURE 4.2

Ullastret (Gerona), view of town across lake formed by floods (1959)

south of Ampurias (see map, Fig. 4.1). Here, since 1947, Miguel Oliva has been excavating, with a few expert and interested workmen and students, the walls, houses, streets, agorá, and temple, and making rich finds which illuminate our picture of Iberian culture. The town rises on a hill 133 feet above sea level, between a river and what was in antiquity a lake (Fig. 4.2).

The most conspicuous remains of Iberian Ullastret, when Oliva started to dig, were the walls, 16 feet high and 12 feet thick, and towers, some round (Fig. 4.3), some square, which ran north and south for 1,450 feet on the unprotected side of the hill (see plan, · Fig. 4.4) and would be even more impressive if they had not been robbed in mediaeval and modern times for church- and road-building. The wall is built of squared blocks from a nearby quarry. They range downwards in size from four by two-and-a-half feet, the courses narrowing as they rise, and are beautifully finished on the outer face, with weep-holes for drainage; some of them, from an earlier building, bear letters in the Iberian alphabet. The towers average about 100 feet— an ancient bow-shot—apart; access to them was by an inner stair leading to a terrace. There is no bond between the round towers and the curtain wall, which means that the towers must have been built first (as early as the sixth century B.C., to judge by the potsherds found within them) and the curtains later (fourth century, by the same criteria). The square towers are later still. There are two main

FIGURE 4.3
Ullastret, round towers of wall

gates and two posterns. Across one of the gates (Fig. 4.5) Oliva found a rough wall, showing signs of hasty construction, as if built in a last-ditch defense. Near the wall he found spear points and huge piles of smooth river pebbles, the size of hens' eggs; these were sling bullets. Since none of his finds were later than the late third or early second centuries B.C., he inferred that Ullastret was destroyed, by Hannibal or Cato, between 218 and 195 B.C. The inner face of the wall shows signs of burning (Fig. 4.6). From the main gate a street leads to the acropolis, whose small (20 by 22 feet) Hellenistic temple was robbed of its stones in the Middle Ages to build the hermitage of Sant Andreu, now incorporated into the small but beautifully arranged

FIGURE 4.4
Ullastret, plan. The "Zona en excavación" has now been excavated. North is at the left

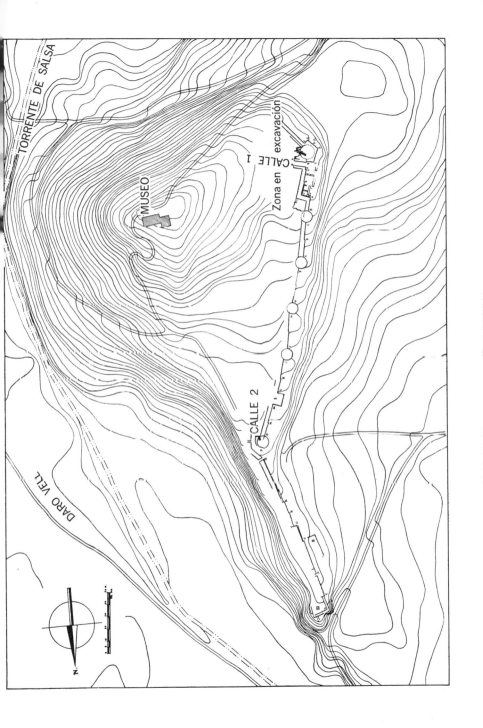

TORRENTE DE SALSA

MUSEO

Zona en excavación

CALLE 1

CALLE 2

DARO VELL

N

FIGURE 4.5
Ullastret, main gate

local museum. Among the finds from the temple were terracotta votive figurines and grotesque apotropaic masks to ward off the evil eye. The temple had a cistern within, for there was no spring within the walls, so that a number of reservoirs were necessary,

FIGURE 4.6
Ullastret, inner face of wall, which shows traces of burning

FIGURE 4.7

*Ullastret, cistern, lined with hydraulic
cement*

scattered about the town (Fig. 4.7); in one of them was found the
altar that once stood in front of the temple. Along the line of the
temple wall an erosion line marked the drip of rain water from the
roof, long since perished, except for a single sandstone cornice block;
thus Oliva could calculate the overhang of the eaves. A spiral decoration from the temple was found built into the emergency wall across
the main gate. The Hellenistic temple must have been at least par-
tially dismantled to get stone to bar the gate, but it was probably
rebuilt and visited by the faithful down into late Roman times; it was
these visitors, Oliva thinks, who dropped the coins, of Claudius (A.D.
41–54), Trajan (A.D. 98–117), and Claudius Gothicus (A.D. 268–
270), found along its approaches.

Beneath the emergency gate-barrier Oliva found a terracotta bull
with an inscription in the Iberian alphabet. Elsewhere, he found
coins from Iberian mints with Iberian inscriptions. Thanks to work
done since 1922 by the brilliant M. Gomez-Moreno, he was able to
transcribe these, though not to translate them, for the Iberians spoke
a language which, like Etruscan and Minoan A, is not Indo-European.
Gomez-Moreno also had had inscriptions and coins to work with.
Starting with the inscriptions, he noticed that the signs Λ   and
   Ν   occurred with the highest frequency: these were likely to be

vowels. Turning to the coins, he noticed that one from Bilbilis (birthplace of the poet Martial) was inscribed   Γ Λ Γ Λ Ν ϟ
where Γ must stand for BI, Λ for L, Ν tor I (thus con-
firming his observation from the inscriptions about frequency and
vowels), and ϟ for S. This was an important breakthrough: it
established that each Iberian sign had to stand for either a vowel
(a Greek invention), liquids and sibilants, or syllabic signs (like
Phoenician, Cypriote, and—he guessed nine years before its deci-
pherment—Linear B); the Iberian alphabet was made up of a
series of separate signs for each of the three categories. Coins
from Emporion—which Oliva also found at Ullastret—were inscribed
as follows: ↑ Ν Ⴗ ᐸ ϟ Ⱶ Ν . This could hardly be a letter-for-
letter transcription of 'the Greek name, but Gomez-Moreno remem-
bered that the name for the indigenous town was Indika. ↑ could
not = I; that letter was already established as Ν . He tried U ,
 Ν then = N, Ⴗ = DI, ᐸ = another syllabic sign, probably CE, ϟ = S (as in archaic Greek alphabets), Ⱶ , standing
between a consonant and a nasal—for he had already guessed Ν
= N—had to be a vowel, probably E; the whole word worked out as
U-N-DI-CE-S-E-N, and he had established that the Iberians had separate single signs for nasals as well as for vowels, liquids and sibilants,
and syllables. He was able to work out equivalents for the other
syllabic signs by starting from the premise that a syllabic sign could
not have a vowel sign *after* it, nor a liquid, sibilant, or nasal *before*
it. Finally he worked out a complete series of equivalents, as follows:

Δ	Ⱶ	Ν	Η	↑		Λ	◁,◊	ϟ,Μ	Ν,Υ	Ⴞ		Ι	⟨	Γ	✦	◻
A	E	I	O	U		L	R	S	N	M		BA	BE	BI	BO	BU

⩔	ᐸ	ʃ	ⵝ	◇		Χ	◈	Ⴗ	ш	Δ	Τ
CA	CE	CI	CO	CU		DA	DE	DI	DO	DU	?

To add to the complications, Iberian exhibits three different sets of
symbols: one in south Portugal, another in Andalucia, and a third in

the Levant, Catalonia, and the Ebro Valley (Iberia proper). Of these the first and possibly the second are the script of a colonizing group (Tartessians?) which first influences indigenous writing and then disappears. The influence is Near Eastern—some of the signs occur much earlier in Linear A and B, and in Cypriote; the final alphabet, which Oliva found in Ullastret, is the indigenous adaptation of an imported system.

So far, we can translate only the symbols on coins from known cities; that is, we can read only transcriptions in the Iberian alphabet of place names which are either non-Iberian (Bilbilis) or Iberian known from literary sources (Indika). The inscriptions will defy translation until a bilingual text turns up. The reader may like to try his hand on the inscription on the Ullastret bull. Transcribed in accordance with Gomez-Moreno's equivalents, it reads:

N E I DI N I U L S DI R ᛜᛒᛜ�;N ᛜ↑⋀ ⌇ᗐ◁

EI . CU L N I E . . . . . . .R ᛒN . ◇⋀N Nᛒ . . . . . ◁

BA L BI . N CO E I E GI A R A R A GIR I ⋀Γ . N ⵊᛒNᛒ ᛍ ⵊ ⋀ ◊⵿ ◊ ⋀ ᛍ ◁

. R . L GI A U S R I . R . . ◊ . ⋀ ᛍ ⋀ ↑ ⵊ ◊ N . ◊ .

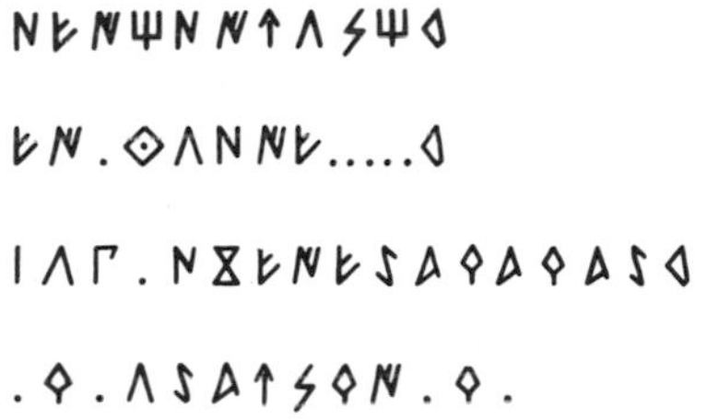

This inscription was found in what Oliva calls Level III. He has illustrated his levels in the museum, in a case illustrated as Figure 4.8. The pottery may be identified as follows:

I	Campanian B	second century B.C.
II	Campanian A	third-second centuries B.C
III	Iberian	fourth century B.C.
IV	Greek red-figure	fifth century B.C.
V	Greek black-figure	sixth century B.C.
VI	Hallstatt, La Tène I	sixth century B.C.
VII	Urnfield	sixth century B.C.
VIII	Ampurian gray ware	sixth century B.C.
IX	unidentified white-on-pink	

FIGURE 4.8
*Ullastret, site museum,
pottery arranged to show
stratigraphy*

These are the levels in the street which crosses the Acropolis street just inside the wall (Fig. 4.9). To the right, the cross-street leads to a modest agorá where Oliva found the stone bases for a portico which must have been of wood; the wooden columns have not survived.

Ullastret's houses are built of stone, without mortar, 20 to 33 feet square. Seventy of them contained "silos," underground pits where grain was stored; Oliva found amphoras filled with wheat, barley, rye, and maize, carbonized in the fire that finally destroyed the town. One house contained so many Greek and Iberian amphoras that it must have been a shop or warehouse. The amphoras and other pottery, along with coins, help to date the houses between the fourth and the early second centuries B.C.

There is so much fine Greek pottery—Phocaean, Attic black- and red-figured—that Oliva is tempted to think of Ullastret as originally a Greek colony, perhaps named Cypsela, which the Iberians later took over; but Greek Emporion is within eyeshot, only nine miles away, and the townsfolk could easily have gotten their Greek pottery from there. Trade relations with Emporion are attested by a number of Ampuritan coins of the third and early second centuries B.C. Dates and economic data are also provided by coins of Ibiza (236 B.C.), Carthage (236–206 B.C.), and Rome (an uncial *as*, a bronze coin worth about a cent, first minted in the Second Punic War, 218–202 B.C.).

The finds from Ullastret, apart from the precious Greek vases, have little intrinsic value, but much documentary worth; they give us insight into the activities of the men, women, and children of the town. The men used the iron chain links, daggers, curved swords (for which Iberians were famous), and hoes. The women busied themselves with the loom weights, spindles, molds for making needles, handmills, and mortars; and beautified themselves with the blue glass paste bracelets

FIGURE 4.9

Ullastret, cross street and houses, southwestern quarter

and hairpins bearing the head of Janus in the same material, as well as with bronze fibulas, rings, and earrings. The children played with the toy vases. The lamp with the faun's head lighted an Iberian house; the key unlocked an Iberian door. The figurine of the grotesque dwarf-god Bes, with his luxuriant beard, leopard's tail, and bandy legs, watched over the birth of their children; they used the incense burner in the shape of the head of Demeter when they prayed for the fertility of their crops. Bes is Egyptian, and Demeter Greek; in religion, these Iberians were not culture-bound.

A stretch of wall, the remains of a humble temple, an inscribed terracotta bull, the ruins of houses, a vast number of potsherds, a few coins, some objects of personal use—these are the pieces of a jigsaw puzzle which, fitted together by archaeologists like Oliva, make up a tiny part of the emerging picture of what life was like in Iberian Spain 72 generations ago.

Ullastret gives an impression of rusticity, simplicity, sobriety. Spanish archaeologists know that Iberians were not always so. One of the sources of their knowledge is a set of over 250 pieces of sculpture unearthed in 1860 near a Roman temple at Cerro de los Santos (Montalegre [Albacete]); the "Hill of the Saints" got its name from the finds, which the local inhabitants thought resembled the statues in their churches. Indeed, there are striking parallels between Iberian sculpture and the twelfth-century Romanesque work of Maestro Mateo. Another Spaniard, Pablo Picasso, has attested to the impact made upon him by the non-academic quality of Cerro de los Santos sculpture. It shows in "Les Demoiselles d'Avignon," the portrait of Gertrude Stein, and the Guernica bulls. The total number of pieces is greater than the total found at Olympia or Delphi, and the quality of some of them falls not far below Greek work: this is native, non-academic Spanish classicism, the only genuine classicism Spain has. Ten years after the statues were discovered, a watchmaker from nearby Yecla, no doubt inspired by his Iberian ancestors, produced some imitative pieces of his own which were bought for the Museo Arqueológico Nacional in Madrid; except where he tried his hand at inventing inscriptions, or altering attitudes or symbols, it is hard to tell the genuine from the fake. At the Paris Exposition of 1878, all the pieces sent from Cerro de los Santos were treated as spurious and relegated to a corner labeled "modern." But a modern critic, J.A. Gaya

FIGURE 4.10
*Madrid, Musoo Arqueológico Nacional,
Gran Dama Oferente,
from Cerro de los Santos*

Nuño, calls the Cerro de los Santos sculpture "the purest, noblest, and most humanistic chapter in the history of Iberian art." He bases his judgment mainly on the masterpiece of the collection, the Gran Dama Oferente (Fig. 4.10), now in the Archaeological Museum in Madrid. She is carved out of a single block, only 4 feet 4 inches tall. Greek in inspiration are her almond eyes, stylized hair, the formal folds of her mantle, and her hieratic expression; but her dress and accessories are Iberian. She is young and beautiful, but she takes her duties as priestess seriously. She wears an elaborate diadem with rosettes from which hang twisted fillets, representing gold; from the fillets depend richly decorated discs. The innermost of her three tunics is fastened at the throat with a T-shaped brooch. She wears three heavy necklaces; she is almost overwhelmed by the weight of it all. She is sacred, severe, distant, untouchable, as she performs her ancestral rite, the pouring of a libation of milk or wine. There is maturity and sureness of touch in the way the sculptor has given the impression of internal tension. Compared with her, the other figures

FIGURE 4.11
Madrid, Museo Arqueológico Nacional, figurines from Cerro de los Santos

FIGURE 4.12
Madrid, Museo
Arqueológico Na-
cional, head of
maiden, from
Cerro de los Santos

are secondary: pilgrims, for the spot was a center for pilgrimage,
like Santiago de Compostela or Fatima later, and it does not take
much effort to imagine the dozens of figures—some of them squat
peasant types (Fig. 4.11), one a wide-eyed innocent maid, like a Virgin on a mediaeval cathedral (Fig. 4.12)—to imagine them, solemn in
their finery, making their pious way in throngs to the temple and
standing or seated there, incarnating even in their peasant crudeness
the human desire for eternity.

Cerro de los Santos is not the only site where Iberian sculpture has
been found. From the fill of the Roman wall of Osuna, some 60
miles east of Seville, comes a series of reliefs of which the best tech-
nically is the horn player (Fig. 4.13). He raises a question of date,
which is moot for all Iberian sculpture because at the time it was
found no attention was paid anywhere—in Spain, France, Italy, or

FIGURE 4.13
Madrid, Museo Arque-
ológico Nacional, horn-
player, from Osuna, ancient
Urso, showing Roman influ-
ence on Iberian art

Greece—to the context of a find; it was an *objet d'art*, a piece to sell
to a museum or an art dealer; the potsherds found with the object,
so precious for dating, were commonly thrown away. Now the Osuna
horn player looks Roman—he wears Roman greaves—and we might
think of him as an Iberian mercenary in Roman service. Osuna,
Roman Urso, was established as a colony by Julius Caesar in 44 B.C.;
and the colony's charter, handsomely engraved on bronze, is in the
Archaeological Museum in Madrid along with the reliefs. But does that
mean that all of this school of sculpture is of Roman date? Some
authorities think so, and the horn player almost certainly is (Gaya
Nuño points out that the later an Iberian piece is, the prouder Span-

iards can be of the resiliency of their Iberian heritage). But surely the Gran Dama Oferente is earlier. She is not Greek enough in feeling to be dated in the fifth century b.c.; but she *is* archaizing in style, and the richness of her dress and ornament has parallels in Greek Sicily of the fourth century. This is probably where she belongs; the Iberian resistance to Roman canons of taste kept Iberian sculptors producing recognizably Iberian work for 350 years, and right through the Roman occupation down to Augustus' time.

The Gran Dama Oferente is a masterpiece, but the Spaniards have taken a greater masterpiece, the Dama de Elche (Fig. 4.14), to their hearts. She was found in the summer of 1897 by workmen leveling ground to plant pomegranate trees at La Alcudia near Elche (Alicante)—an oasis of palm trees, orange and lemon groves, in a blinding light like that of North Africa. Displayed on the balcony of the lucky finder, she became a nine-day wonder, but only that, for she went almost at once into a long exile. Pierre Paris, discoverer of the Osuna reliefs, another of the foreigners entranced with Spain—like Breuil, Schulten, and Siret—exchanged a series of code telegrams with the Louvre; the proprietor of the land on which the Dama was found, exasperated at the bureaucratic delays of the Spanish authorities, sold her to the French for 4,000 francs; and in the Louvre she remained until in 1941 General Pétain sent her back, along with the Osuna pieces, to General Franco. She now occupies a place of honor in Madrid, not in the Archaeological Museum but in the Prado, where she ranks in importance with those other purely Spanish treasures, the paintings of El Greco, Velásquez, and Goya.

The Dama is a sandstone bust 22 inches high; the lips, mantilla, and cloak, originally painted red, which over the centuries turned to a brown patina, faded still further in the more humid air of France. As a Spanish lady should, she wears a high comb and mantilla, and is richly bejeweled: a diadem; over her ears, suspended by a double strap, hang sumptuous discs, their edges decorated with an alternating pattern of triple globes and quadrifoils (the girls of Valencia still wear such ornaments, hollow to contain braided hair). Between the discs and her ears she wears double-voluted plaques from which are suspended fillets ending in acorn—or amphora-like—knobs. Over her mantilla she wears a shawl fastened in front by a large Iberian brooch. The shawl conceals the shoulder supports for the heavy discs. Her three heavy necklaces have amphora-ornaments probably intended to represent gold filigree.

There are Greek, Punic, and Iberian parallels for this baroque jewelry, which is magnificent, even ostentatious, indicating great wealth. However, the face is not plutocratic, but aristocratic; block out the bizarre ornament, and you have the essence of harmonious, noble, proud womanhood. The sculptor who could bring out the contrast between the rococo taste in jewelry and the sad, severe face was nothing short of a genius. Naturally, most Spanish art historians (García y Bellido excepted) would like to claim her as Iberian, as their own. There is not much help one way or the other in the vague reports of the context in which she was found, in front of a sort of triptych of stone slabs in a Roman house; she may well be an heirloom of much earlier date, probably, like the Gran Dama Oferente —whose jewelry is of the same style—fourth century b.c. But whatever the origin of her inspiration, the Spanish people have taken her for their own. She is the acknowledged First Lady of Spanish sculpture.

Iberian sculptors liked to carve animals as well as human figures: their bulls (Fig. 4.15) and monsters (Fig. 4.16)—both in the Archaeological Museum, Madrid—meant as much to them as dolphins and centaurs to the Greeks. The Bicha de Balazote (Fig. 4.15), found in the late nineteenth century, is an independent Iberian version of the man-headed bulls on the coins of Gela in Greek Sicily. The body, with its subtle observations of the curves of the tucked-under hoofs and of the tail ready to whisk away flies, is Iberian, the head is archaizing Greek in inspiration. The Lion of Baeza (Jaén) shows the influence of wood carving technique, and the toothy vigilance and controlled force so much admired in African art. This sculpture may have religious or totemic significance, but the sculptors felt, too, a natural attraction to the animals they knew and loved. At Cigarralejo (Murcia) were found over 200 carved stone horses, votive offerings to intercede with the gods to keep the beasts in health. Iberian animal sculpture can only be dated by style, since no record was kept of the context of their finding. The consensus seems to be that the Bull of Balazote is fifth century b.c., others not earlier than the third century b.c., a survival of traditional archaic techniques. As a whole, Iberian sculpture is memorable as the work of men who wanted to exalt all that pulsed with life in the Spanish countryside, in the process serving gods and men and respecting and ennobling animals. Gaya Nuño has well called it "a chapter in the aesthetic inquietude of Spain."

FIGURE 4.14
Madrid, Prado, Dama de Elche

FIGURE 4.15
Madrid, Museo Arqueológico Nacional, Bull of Balazote

FIGURE 4.16
Madrid, Museo Arqueológico Nacional, "Lion" of Baeza

The finest examples of Iberian pottery come from the town of Azaila (Teruel), near the Ebro, 36 miles southeast of Zaragoza. The excavation here was begun in 1919 by J. Cabré, the same man who published the pottery. The acropolis, on a low rise 800 feet by 400 feet, was strategically so defensible that Loyalist troops occupied it during the Spanish Civil War; archaeologists on the side of General Franco's "Movimiento Glorioso" complained bitterly of the damage the Loyalists did.

Cabré found that the acropolis was defended by a moat 20 feet deep and tapering from 36 feet wide at the top to 13 feet wide at the bottom, which was paved with pebbles. A drawbridge crossed the moat; beyond it (see model, Fig. 4.17) climbed three ramps, paved with curbs and sidewalks.

The left ramp passed two temples, one Iberian and one Roman. The inhabitants destroyed the Iberian temple to make a barricade for a last-ditch defense, as at Ullastret; Cabré found in it a fine rosetted bronze bull's head on an alabaster pedestal. The other temple is called Roman because two bronze heads found in it have been identified as Augustus and Livia, in which case the temple was in use after the town was sacked. But Cabré reports the workmanship as Iberian. It is a small building (13 by 21 feet), smaller than the temple at Ullastret, with adobe walls stuccoed on the outside to imitate squared

FIGURE 4.17
Madrid, Museo Arqueológico Nacional, Azaila, model

blocks close-fitted at the edges. The outer paving was of sandstone, the threshold of pine. The cella floor was mosaic in a black and white swastika pattern on a red ground. The columns were Tuscan (plain, like Doric, but without fluting); the architectural décor—triglyphs, metopes, pediment, and interior cornices—was again in stucco imitating stone. The altar was *inside* the temple, which is most unusual. Beside it, Cabré found a carbonized catapult of the Ampurias type: the gods of Azaila apparently did not fight on the side of their native worshipers. Many fine Iberian vases were found in the temple, and the fragments of a horse, larger than life, in bronze.

The second ramp led from the drawbridge to watchtowers overlooking the fields in all directions. The third ramp led to a paved street which followed the inside of the wall all around. Here to the right was the market quarter, connected by stairs in three directions to the upper part of the acropolis. Azaila did not have open housing; the commercial classes were segregated from the official and military element.

The houses were rectangular in plan, of one or two stories, of stone in their lower courses, adobe above. The roofs were of logs covered with branches and daubed with clay; the kitchen sinks were of alabaster. The lower-class houses had pantries at the back; the chiefs' houses had a separate storeroom at the street door; both were found filled with Iberian pottery, set in stands.

To the south, Cabré found the wall breached; the enemy had used the fall of stones from the wall to fill in the moat; a large number of stone catapult balls and lead sling-bullets found here confirm the hypothesis of a desperate defense at this point.

The miscellaneous finds included bronze horse's head finials for furniture, a bronze lamp in the shape of a Negro's head, a bronze ladle, a scale with bronze weights in the shape of swans' heads, a silver-inlaid belt buckle. Several hoards of coins turned up, mostly Iberian; one lot from the water tower under the access stair contained 601 coins; another lot, of 112, was found in a kitchen. No coins were found that dated after Sertorius' uprising of 78–74 B.C., and no Roman pottery of the Arretine type, which dates from the early years of Augustus. The acropolis was burned three times and restored twice. The archaeologists disagree about when the fires occurred; the latest guess would date the first conflagration about 195 B.C., in Cato's time; the second between 80 and 75 B.C. (Sertorius); and the third after the battle of Lérida, in 49 B.C., after which the acropolis was not

rebuilt, though worshipers may still, as we saw, have frequented the
Roman temple.

The characteristic Iberian pottery can be assigned to these three
periods. The earliest is abstract, filling the field of the vase with
volute tree-of-life designs (Fig. 4.18), stylized, in the style of a painter
sure of his medium. The second style has human figures, like the rider
with lance, a fallen warrior beneath his horse (Fig. 4.19). In the

FIGURE 4.20

Barcelona, Museo Arqueológico
Provincial: Oliva, warrior vase,
illustrating Iberian third style

FIGURE 4.21

Elche, vase illustrating Iberian
baroque decoration

latest style, human figures cram the field, as in the warrior vase, not
from Azaila but from Oliva (Valencia), yet in the same style (Fig.
4.20) with the field crammed with martial figures, painted in with a
fantastic *horror vacui*—an instinct to leave not an inch of the vase
undecorated, shown also in a vase from Elche (Fig. 4.21). Though
there are Greek parallels from the seventh century B.C.—the volutes

from Melos, the animals from Rhodes, the human figures from Sicily—no one would ever mistake an Iberian vase for a Greek one. The painters, like the sculptors, impressed their own personality on their work; some Azaila pots are even signed.

The dates are controversial. Beltrán would assign all the pottery to the four generations between Cato and Sertorius; i.e., 195–75 B.C. There is general agreement that the stylized curves came first, though they are by no means primitive; the beasts next; and the "baroque" human figures last.

The illustrations are inadequate to suggest the richness of Iberian painting. Taken as a whole, the vases present a vivid cross section of Iberian life: bullfights, horse taming, magic, folk dancing; and a colorful picture of the fantastic and inventive Iberian taste in décor: stars, rosettes, meanders, cruciform flowers, fern-leaves, wheels, spirals, concentric circles, zigzags, swastikas. And the abstractions can turn into animals, or vice versa; swastikas into bulls, bulls into swastikas. There are bulls on wheels, and bulls with fishes' heads. Like the sculpture, Iberian painting contrives to be complex and rustic, both at once. Iberian art is not simply a provincial degeneration of Greek, just as El Greco was something more than a Cretan. His originality, like Picasso's, has Iberian roots.

Between 800 and 600 B.C. waves of Indo-European-speaking Celts, escaping the cold climate—as they do still—came over the Pyrenees and settled more or less peacefully in northwest Spain and Portugal. Intermarrying with the Iberians, they produced the Celtiberian stock, *robur Hispaniae*—"Spanish hearts-of-oak"—the Romans called them, and with reason, for with tenacity and courage, in their mountain fastnesses, they held out for generations against the Roman occupation.

Their hilltop towns, called *citânias* or *castros*, are most numerous in northern Portugal. From his study window in Guimarães the Portuguese archaeologist F. Martins Sarmento, who began to excavate the Citânia de Briteiros in 1875, could see no less than six *castros*; a modest estimate gives the Portuguese total at more than 5,000.

No great ancient historian took any notice of the *castros*, but the Greek geographer Strabo, writing under Augustus, speaks appreciatively of Celtiberian or Lusitanian virtues: loyalty to their plighted word, love of freedom, bitter antagonism to foreign authority, pride, hospitality, ready response to friendly treatment, stubbornness, simplicity, clannishness. Their warriors, whom they represented in crude

statues (Fig. 4.22), leading marauding bands, held Roman consular
armies at bay; Viriathus, a symbol to the Portuguese like Vercingetorix
to the French and Arminius to the Germans, over 16 years, 154–138
B.C., killed 20,000 Romans before he was finally treacherously murdered.

The Citânia de Briteiros rises behind its triple wall (see aerial photograph, Fig. 4.23) on a hill 1,083 feet high, 9 miles north of
Guimarães, magnificently overlooking a country of fertile valleys and
forested hills, between the Douro and the Minho rivers. The excavated area, 812 by 487 feet, contains about 150 stone houses, some
round, some oval, some square; Martins Sarmento reconstructed two
of the round ones (Fig. 4.24); his work has been carried on by Col.
Mario Cardozo. A typical ground plan of a *castro* house, with its characteristic porch, can be illustrated from Sanfins, a large, important,
and well-excavated *castro* 15 miles to the southwest (Fig. 4.25).
Beside the houses were corrals, with sliding stone doors and stone
rings for tethering animals (Fig. 4.26, also from Sanfins). The house
doors had decorated jambs (Fig. 4.27, from Áncora, 36 miles northwest, now in the Martins Sarmento Museum, Guimarães). There were
no windows; smoke escaped through vents cut through stone blocks
in a triskeles pattern (Fig. 4.28). Briteiros is unusual among *castros*

FIGURE 4.22
Guimarães, museum,
Lusitanian warriors

FIGURE 4.23
Briteiros, air view

FIGURE 4.24
Briteiros, round houses, reconstruction

FIGURE 4.25
Sanfins, view showing house plan

FIGURE 4.26
Sanfins, wall with stone tether

FIGURE 4.27
Guimarães, Museo Martins Sarmento, stone doorway, from Áncora

FIGURE 4.28
Guimarães, Museo Martins Sarmento, pierced stone air vents, from Briteiros

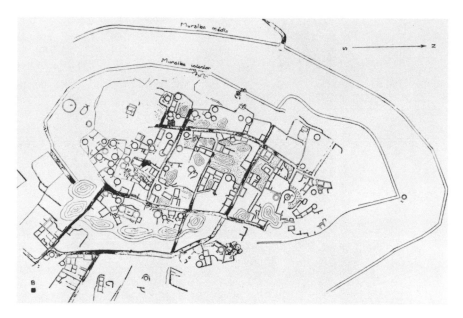

FIGURE 4.29
Briteiros, plan showing grid of streets

in having its houses arranged along streets in a rough grid pattern (see plan, Fig. 4.29). The Portuguese have published no reconstruction drawing, but Briteiros must have looked very like the Spanish *castro* of Coaña (near Navia [Asturias]) as reconstructed by García y Bellido (Fig. 4.30).

The most impressive find from Briteiros is the colossal "Pedra Formosa," over nine feet high and over nine feet wide (Fig. 4.31): it took 24 span of oxen to move it to the Guimarães museum. From the moment of its discovery in 1873 there was widely varied speculation about its purpose. Was it a pediment, a sacrificial stone, or a magic couch lying on which would remove sterility? The question was finally answered in 1930 when another stone of exactly similar shape was found at Briteiros, blocking the entrance of a burial chamber (Fig. 4.32). Through the hole at the bottom offerings could be made to the dead.

Briteiros yielded very little sculpture, and what there is is so crude that it is hard to tell male from female. This is partly because of the obduracy of the material, which is granite; partly because of the remoteness of the spot, beyond the farthest reaches of sophisticated

EL CASTRO ᴅ COAÑA
ANAPARÁSTASIS ᴅᴇʟ BARRIO
EXTRAMVROS

FIGURE 4.30

Coaña (Asturias), reconstruction by García y Bellido, to illustrate typical castro

civilization; but chiefly because the *castro* culture did not feel the same impulse to self-expression as the Iberians. Four examples will illustrate the crude power of this Celtic or Celtiberian sculpture. The first is the Colossus of Pedralva (Fig. 4.33), acquired in 1876 by Martins Sarmiento for his museum in Guimarães. It comes from the bottom of Briteiros hill. It is nearly 10 feet tall, made of three pieces of granite, and there is no mistaking its sex: the phallus is enormous. The other examples are all of animals. One (Fig. 4.34) is on a pedestal in the town square of Murça (Vila Real), 90 miles east and south of Briteiros. It probably represents a wild boar, the totem of a tribe or class. The other two are in Spain, but in the same crude *castro* tradition: a boar from near Ávila (Fig. 4.35) in the garden of the Museo Arqueológico Nacional in Madrid; and the famous Toros de Guisando (Ávila, Fig. 4.36).

As to the dates of the *castro* culture, the British prehistorian Christopher Hawkes dug some trial trenches in 1958 at Sabroso, within eyeshot of Briteiros, a mile and a half southwest, and reported stratigraphic evidence that the *castro* had been in existence for five centuries before the Romans. The oldest other evidence is from coins:

FIGURE 4.31
*Guimarães, Museo
Martins Sarmento,
Pedra Formosa I*

FIGURE 4.32
*Guimarães, Museo
Martins
Sarmento, Pedra
Formosa II*

Roman, of the gens Aurelia (244 B.C.) at both Briteiros and Sabroso; of the gens Porcia (149 B.C.) at Briteiros. Martins Sarmento in 1879 found Iberian coins, unfortunately now lost, and Iberian pottery turned up in the excavations of 1943. More could be done with dating the

FIGURE 4.33

Guimarães, Museo Martins Sarmento, Colossus of Pedralva

fibulae and the pottery stamps. The very existence of stamped pottery—*terra sigillata*, or Arretine ware—takes us into Roman times (as late as 30 B.C.), and there are some later pieces which were imported from Gaul. Coins take us down still later. They come from Roman *municipia* like Bilbilis (Calatayud [Zaragoza]), Gracchuris (founded in 179 B.C. by the father of the tribune Tiberius Gracchus, modern Alfaro [Logroño]), and Calagurris (birthplace of Quintilian, famous professor of rhetoric under the Emperor Domitian [A.D. 81–96]); modern Calahorra (Logroño); Emerita (Mérida [Badajoz], capital of the Roman province of Lusitania from 25 B.C., see Chapter 6); and Ebora (Évora [Alentejo, Portugal] seat of a famous temple of the third century A.D., see Chapter 7). A hoard discovered in Sanfins in 1950 contained 288 silver denarii ranging in date from 230 to 28 B.C. The latest coin of a Roman emperor found in Briteiros is of Constantine the Great (A.D. 306–337).

FIGURE 4.34
Murça (Vila Real, Portugal), boar

This means that the cultural life of Briteiros lasted from at least the third century B.C. down to the barbarian invasions. From the fact that no swords were found in the excavation, Colonel Cardozo infers that the final abandonment was peaceful. The usual miscellaneous finds— handmills, loom weights, lamps, glassware, beads, compasses, pincers— prove that life went on in Briteiros in the old native tradition, little affected by the Roman invaders. This is what is meant by the Iberian —here we might call it the Celtiberian—resistance. As in Italy the native Villanovans preserved their primitive culture in the face of Etruscan overlords, as in Greece the "Pelasgians" passively resisted the impact of the Greek-speaking invaders of 1900 B.C.,* so on the Iberian peninsula, at Ullastret, Cerro de los Santos, Elche, Azaila, Briteiros, and numberless other places, the indigenous culture doggedly persisted, virile, pure, conservative, indomitable, and independent. To the most glorious chapter in the Iberian struggle for independence we next turn.

---

* See *The Mute Stones Speak,* pp. 13–29, *passim; The Greek Stones Speak,* pp. 32–34 (Eutresis), 38–39 (Lerna).

FIGURE 4.35
Madrid, Museo Arqueológico Nacional, boar from Ávila

FIGURE 4.36
Guisando (Ávila), toros

5

NUMANTIA'S LAST STAND

(133-27 B.C.)

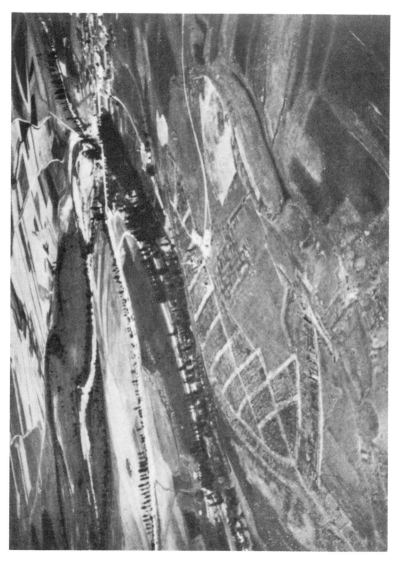

FIGURE 5.1
Numantia, air view

NUMANTIA (FIG. 5.1), THE SYMBOL OF Spain's struggle for independence against the Romans, rises sheer above the River Duero (Fig. 5.2) on the stony, dry, wind-swept plateau of Old Castile, 3,575 feet above sea level, at a strategic crossroad a little more than four miles northeast of the provincial capital of Soria. The surrounding landscape, solemn and grand, with 7,500-foot peaks rising in the distance, is a fit theater for the tragedy that unfolded there in 133 B.C. It is a stark country, haunt of wolves and vultures. Spring does not come till May, summer is short and parching, winter begins in October. To this austere setting Adolf Schulten came to excavate in August of 1905. He stayed for eight seasons, and fell in love with the place: the dark blue evergreens, the pale violet peaks, the various greens of moss, elm, and willow, the tawny plowland, the golden wheat. He spoke of his years there as the happiest time of his life; he writes warmly of the sheer pleasure of dedicating the best years of one's life to a job freely chosen and favored by luck.

The luck began virtually with the first stroke of the pick, for Schulten's workmen hit almost at once upon the burnt layer which divided Roman Numantia (Fig. 5.3) from its heroic Celtiberian predecessor. He found Neolithic axes and pottery, a blank for the Bronze Age, then the evidence of vases and fibulae for what he claimed was a Celtic occupation of about 500 B.C. At this stage the village

FIGURE 5.2
Numantia bridge over River Duero at Garray (foundations Roman)

must have looked very much like Briteiros or Coaña: a collection of 500 to 1,000 straw-thatched huts for a population of 2,000 to 4,000, in a bleak countryside which would not support either the olive or the vine. No one would have come voluntarily to this desolate place; the Celts must have been driven here by warfare of which otherwise we know nothing. They were always cursed by their inability to unify, on which the Romans were to capitalize. But clan names scratched on the pottery show that they were not entirely anarchistic.

At a certain level in his excavation Schulten claimed to notice a change in the pottery style: Iberian motifs began to creep in, and by the appearance in the same level of a few allegedly datable Greek sherds, he dated the intrusion about 300 B.C. Since there were no signs of sack or burning in this level, and since Celtic names persisted in the vase graffiti, he assumed a case of peaceful fusion. But not without change: the Iberians, he said, remodeled Numantia on a grid plan, with rectangular blocks, ten streets one way, two the other, plus a street that encircled the town just inside the wall; the whole looked not unlike Greco-Iberian Emporion. In this phase Numantia had some 1,500 houses, which implies a population of 6,000 or more, living in an area of about 55 acres, behind a wall 20 feet thick, made in two faces of unworked stone with a rubble fill; in some places the townsfolk had allowed the wall to crumble. There were gates at the east and south, with plazas beside them. The road inside the wall varied from 10 to 16 feet in width and had sidewalks and steppingstones; they still show wagon ruts 2,000 years old. The houses were rectangular, averaging 40 feet long by 10 feet wide, the long side facing the street. They were built of unworked stone below, adobe above, with roofs probably of branches and clay: Schulten found no roof tiles in the Celtiberian levels. There were no windows. They commonly had three rooms, which the household animals shared, as in remote parts of Spain and Portugal today. The kitchens had stone sinks; some houses had stone-lined holes for storage under them, as at Ullastret.

Neither Schulten nor the Spanish archaeologists who excavated after him found the remains of any public buildings: the town was poor and primitive; its inhabitants worshiped not in temples but in sacred groves—lofty Moncayo was their sacred mountain. From the skulls (probably trophies; the cemetery of Numantia has never been

FIGURE 5.3
Roman Numantia, plan

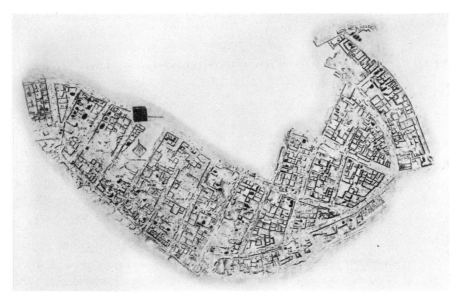

found), Schulten deduced that the stock was mainly Iberian, narrow-headed, and (from the likenesses on the painted vases, of which there are over 800 among the 13,815 objects in the Soria Museo Numantino) short, dark, and wiry, agile in the dance and in guerrilla warfare, strong enough to cope with the climate and the isolation. The women wore the *mantilla* (Fig. 5.4), and the men a tunic, short trousers, plaid, and long hair. From the bones of stag, boar, and rabbit found in the houses, Schulten inferred that the Numantine diet was mainly game (which gave the pasta-eating Romans dysentery). In default of wine, they drank mead. They brushed their teeth with urine, whose cleansing properties modern toothpaste manufacturers have only recently rediscovered.

The painted pottery shows their interests: in horse taming (Fig. 5.5), warfare, duels, dancing, and religion. The bull was a sacred animal (as still). The earliest phase of the pottery is naturalistic; a middle phase features monsters; only in the final phase did the excavators find stylized representations of the human figure. Schulten dated this pottery 300–133 B.C.; the latest excavator, F. Wattenberg (1963; died 1967), dated it all 133–29 B.C. and reported no evidence of habitation before 133 B.C. in the excavated area. Only further scientific excavation will clear up the contradiction.

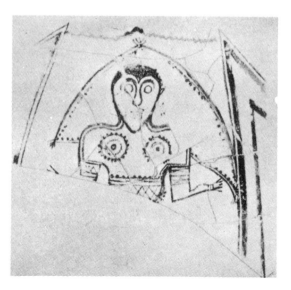

FIGURE 5.4
*Soria, Museo
Numantino, vase
showing woman in
mantilla*

Such, Schulten thought, was the Numantia which the Romans laid siege to. Schulten was interested in Numantia, as later he was to be interested in Tartessus, for the light which he hoped excavation would throw upon history. He was particularly drawn to Numantia because he held a lifelong brief for underdogs; he loved the Spanish for having—as he said with some manipulation of history—stood off the Romans for 250 years, while the Gauls held out for only 10. But it is perfectly true that in the 10 years before 133 B.C., Rome lost 65,000 citizen-soldiers in Spain, and, in the whole period of the Spanish resistance, 218–27 B.C., between 150,000 and 200,000. The Spanish wars bled Rome white; no Roman, officer or man, ever really wanted to fight in Spain. Schulten argued that the Spanish wars brought on the Gracchan revolution in Rome, the aim of which was to restore the property qualification on which service in the old Roman army depended. He saw Spain as the training ground of future dictators: Marius served in the Numantine campaign; both Caesar and Pompey earned—or at least claimed—laurels there; and later Caesar defeated Pompeian armies in the northeast and south; the final pacification was the work of Octavian-Augustus. So, as Schulten did, we must review some history in order to make what the spade uncovers meaningful.

FIGURE 5.5
Soria, Museo Numantino,
vase showing horse-taming

The Romans in Spain had the disadvantage of overextended communications. The voyage from Italy to Tarragona took a month or more; then two weeks for the overland journey from there up the Ebro Valley to Numantia, through country made-to-order for guerrillas. In the hot, dry summers the legions could march only at night, and could find little or no water. In the spring and fall, torrential rains made both roads and rivers impassable. The countryside was too poor to supply the necessary fodder or transport; there was neither oil nor wine, without which life for an Italian is impossible. Winter cut off campaigning altogether. On the high plateau of Old Castile, the northeast wind was strong enough to knock over a legionary soldier, even weighed down by his 50-pound pack. The enemy, on the other hand, was used to the terrain, the climate, and the poverty. All he had to do was unite, persevere, and avoid pitched battles and sieges. The Spanish lost because of intertribal feuds, weariness, and letting themselves be trapped inside the walls of Numantia; at their own kind of warfare, they whipped the Romans at will.

As we saw, it was the Spanish mines that enticed the Romans to Spain, just as the mines of Mexico and Peru were to attract the Spaniards to Mexico and Peru 1,700 years later. To exploit, the Romans had to dominate; they rationalized the attempt at dominion as legitimate defense of allies. An uprising brought Cato to Old Castile in 195 B.C.; Schulten found his solidly-constructed winter quarters at Renieblas. Tiberius Gracchus' father beat the Celtiberians in 179 B.C., and claimed to have taken 300 "cities." But he was one of the few Romans whose good faith the Spanish trusted; the result was a 25-year peace, until 154 B.C. Gracchus founded, on the Ebro 42 miles northeast of Numantia, a Roman colony, Gracchuris (nowadays Alfaro, in the province of Logroño). It was the first to bear the name of a Roman general.

In 153 B.C., disputes over tribute and the furnishing of troops sparked into flame the Celtiberian War, which was to last 20 years and end with the destruction of Numantia. (Up to now the Roman official year had begun on March 1; in 153 B.C. it was changed to January 1 to give the consular generals time to get to Spain to open the campaigning season early. Thus our celebration of New Year's has Spanish origins.) The consul let himself be ambushed, and lost 6,000 men. Three weeks later, near Numantia, his elephants stampeded, and he lost again, this time 4,000 men. Since Rome was at least six weeks away, he could expect no reinforcements; preferring not to confess defeat by withdrawal, he wintered in Renieblas, only three and a half miles away, where Cato had camped 42 years before.

Schulten found and excavated the Renieblas encampments (Fig. 5.6). No earlier ones have been found anywhere; they document 200 years of conflict. Schulten's first campaign at Numantia had been so successful that the Spanish decided to take over; he chivalrously withdrew, and devoted himself to excavation in the environs. Nineteenth-century excavators had mistaken the walls at Renieblas for corrals, and unsuspecting hunters from Soria had been using the ruins as partridge blinds. Schulten discovered the camps in the fall of 1908, and dug there for the next four seasons in the midst of a great, silent, wooded mountain solitude where once arms clashed and trumpets blew. Nobilior's proved to be the best-preserved of the five camps he found; its plan (Fig. 5.7) was visible without excavation; it comes the closest of all to the rectangular plan for the canonical Roman camp described by the Greek historian Polybius, who at the age of 70 was present with the Roman general Scipio the Younger at the siege of Numantia in 133 B.C.

Surveyors laid out the camp on a grid plan, with the general's headquarters, the *praetorium*, in the center, at the highest point (1,280 feet), within eyeshot of Numantia, so that there was no chance of surprise from that quarter. The site of the camp was handy to two streams, and to woods for timber. The camp measured approximately 2,400 feet each way, with stone walls 10 feet thick along the escarpment and a sheer drop from the outer face. The walls were provided with artillery towers at intervals; there were flanking towers at the gates. The main gate, on the north, opened onto the Via Principalis, 100 feet wide; it allowed space for formations, addresses to the troops, punishments, and executions; Schulten found in this street quarters for the *tribuni militum* (colonels commanding); there was also provision for latrines. The Italian allies—auxiliary troops —had inferior barracks just inside the main gate; the Iberian auxiliaries, who were not trusted, were housed in separate extramural barracks to the east. Each barracks held 120 men; each barracks had a connecting wing for 20 beasts of burden; the 10 elephants,

FIGURE 5.6
Numantia and Renieblas, Roman camps, plan

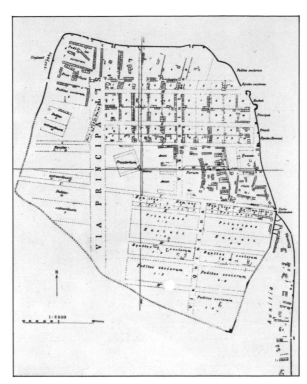

FIGURE 5.7
*Renieblas, Nobi-
lior's camp, plan*

who were considered dangerous, were stabled outside the wall to the
northwest. The six *praefecti* commanding the Italians had com-
modious houses between the barracks.

East of the headquarters was the forum, with shops; farther east
was the *quaestorium*, with offices and storage space for provisions and
baggage. The headquarters building itself was 200 Roman feet on
a side, arranged around a courtyard; Schulten found only its southeast corner; the rest was destroyed by the building of Pompey's camp
in the campaign against Sertorius of 75 and 74 B.C. Between the
headquarters building and the forum were luxurious quarters for the
general's staff with dining rooms found stocked with fine Greek
tableware; only plain ware was found in the troops' quarters. Other
finds included javelins, swords, daggers, arrows (including large ones
for firing from catapults), sling bullets, ballista balls, breastplates,
horses' bits, and harness brasses (but no horseshoes; they had not
yet been invented). The day-to-day life of the camp was illustrated by

storage amphoras for grain, oil, and wine (which must have had to be transported from a great distance), lamps, whetstones, handmills, game counters, and depilatory tweezers. (Twenty years later, Roman sources were to report that Scipio, toughening up his demoralized army, confiscated 20,000 of these evidences of effeminacy.) Schulten also found two hoards of silver coins, one of 120 pieces, the other of 70. The men who hid them, victims of Nobilior's inefficiency, must have been killed in battle; at any rate they never returned to collect their savings.

The winter in Renieblas after Nobilior's defeat before Numantia must have been terrible. Men and beasts starved or were frozen to death: Schulten found pathetic, makeshift hearths in the barracks. Those who died on expeditions for fodder and firewood were cremated in a mass grave he found on the Moñegon road southwest of the camp.

Nobilior handed over to his successor, M. Claudius Marcellus, who made a peace with the Celtiberians in the old liberal Gracchan tradition: it lasted from 151 to 143 B.C. He moved camp from Renieblas to Castillejo (Fig. 5.6) a kilometer north of Numantia. Schulten found the remains of this camp also. It lay under the later camp of Scipio; Schulten identified it by its different orientation and by the different color of the sandstone used in its construction.

In the army of Marcellus' successor was a 34-year-old volunteer who 18 years later was to destroy Numantia. This was Scipio the Younger, cultured, intellectual, a lover of things Greek, friend and patron of creative artists, a man whose destiny it was to be in 146 B.C. to order the destruction of Carthage and to weep over its ruins, foreseeing one day a similar fate for Rome. In this earlier campaign (which did not include Numantia) he distinguished himself for bravery, fighting in single combat with a Celtiberian champion and first over the wall in the successful siege of a Celtiberian town.

When the war broke out again in 143 B.C., its native ringleader was the Lusitanian Viriathus, whom the Portuguese have named their national hero. First a shepherd, then a hunter, then a bandit leader, he made life miserable for the Romans by his successful guerrilla tactics; the legions cowered before his barbaric troops with their long hair and fearsome war cry. But in the end (139 B.C.), the Romans bribed Quislings to assassinate him while he slept. The

Portuguese have made a national monument of an alleged camp of his, the "Cava de Viriato," just north of Viseu (Fig. 5.8), an enormous octagonal earthwork, over 250 yards on a side, embracing over 70 acres. Schulten thought it was not a native stronghold, but a camp of the Roman general Brutus Callaicus, consul in 138 B.C. But the Portuguese, patriots first and archaeologists second, have erected on a granite base just south of the earthwork a bronze statue of Viriathus surrounded by five of his shepherd-guerrillas.

In 134 B.C. Scipio was elected consul; the conqueror of mighty Carthage was sent to blockade and starve out a wretched Celtiberian town. Arriving at Tarragona, he found the morale and discipline of his army at a low ebb. He banished the camp followers and changed luxury to austerity—we remember the confiscation of the depilatory tweezers. He forbade the troops hot baths, made them breakfast standing, and sent them on forced marches, with himself in the rear to prevent desertion. Those who fell out were beaten. The infantry was forbidden to ride horseback and made to carry heavy

FIGURE 5.8
Viseu, Portugal,
"Cava de
Viriato," plan

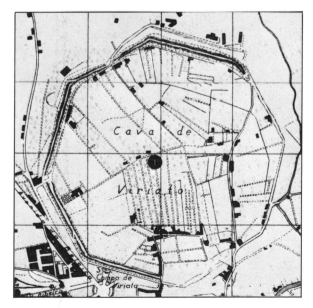

packs. There was practice in the heavy but vitally necessary work of making permanent camps.

On arrival at Numantia, Scipio must have been surprised at the tininess of the town which had held the Romans at bay for 20 years. His trained eye could see that the terrain was made for circumvallation; he determined to surround the town with a ring of camps connected by a wall. Schulten, blocked by the Spaniards from excavating Numantia proper, spent three seasons (1906–1908) exploring Scipio's siege works (Fig. 5.6). He found that their perimeter was nearly five and a half miles, as economical a circuit as the terrain would allow; the troops available would permit them to be manned with three soldiers per meter. The walls, where preserved, measured 16 feet high and 13 feet thick; every 130 feet was a four-story tower for catapults and signaling—a red flag by day, torches by night. Schulten calculated that Scipio's men, working under pressure, could have finished their back-breaking task in ten days. The seven camps themselves were sited a little more than a kilometer apart, for ease in helping each other and to facilitate flanking fire.

Of the seven camps, the two most important were the head-quarters of the commanding general and his legate—who was also his brother—Lucius Fabius Maximus Aemilianus. Scipio chose to camp at Castillejo, north of the beleaguered town, where, as we saw, Marcellus had camped 17 years before. Schulten found great difficulty in getting permission to excavate here; the land was divided among 30 different owners. But once the red tape had been cut, with his usual luck the first wall he hit upon was that of Scipio's *praetorium*. Scipio used the remains of the foundations of Marcellus' camp—which the Numantines had destroyed—as the basis for his own. Castillejo was the site best-suited for a headquarters: it had the best view and was the best-protected. It covered about 18 acres, was roughly pentagonal in shape, and faced east on the axis of the circumvallation, being oriented for sunrise in early October. Schulten found it better built than the other camps; the commander himself had had his eye on the work. Besides, the camp was built of river stone, which is easier to work than the harder limestone of the other camps. The circuit wall was 13 feet thick, the same as the circumvallation; the foundations of the barracks walls were 1 Roman foot thick and 2 Roman feet high; above, they were of adobe, and roofed with boughs held down with stones.

FIGURE 5.9
Numantia, Scipio's camp at Castillejo, cavalry barracks

The *praetorium* measured 120 Roman feet on a side, with a patio open to the east; the style was Greek, as befitted a philhellene like Scipio. Here the commander must have spent many a long winter evening conversing with his staff, which included many of the most distinguished Romans of the present and the future: Marius, the victor (104 B.C.) of the Jugurthine War; his future opponent, the Numidian prince Jugurtha; Gaius Gracchus the reformer, son of the founder of Gracchuris; Lucilius the satiric poet; Rutilius Rufus, philosopher, diarist, and statesman; and two historians: one Roman, Sempronius Asellio, and one Greek, Polybius. We may be sure that Scipio's reputation suffered no harm at their hands. Here in his headquarters Scipio prophesied to Marius a brilliant future, warned Jugurtha not to intrigue against Rome, and talked statecraft with Rutilius Rufus.

The western part of the camp was taken up with barracks, infantry on the north, cavalry on the south (Fig. 5.9); Schulten covered them up again to protect them against destruction by the plow. There were five men to a room, two rows of six pairs of rooms to a barracks; a street ran between. Of the rooms, one of the pair was a dormitory, the other for arms and equipment.

The eastern part of the camp held the Italian troops, and the grain store, identified by its thicker, buttressed walls (it held provisions for 15 or 16 days). To the north, Schulten found four pairs of large buildings which housed the artillery batteries. He calculated that the whole camp would hold at a pinch 5,500 men; the actual complement was more like 2,500. Being smaller than Nobilior's camp at Renieblas, it was easier to defend: its 18 acres were cramped for a legion, which normally required 25.

The finds from the camp were meager, because the land had been worked over for centuries. Schulten reports two silver rings, two silver plaques, two twisted gold-wire pendants, two richly-decorated bronze belt buckles, a bronze ring with the figure of a Cupid, four Iberian and six Roman coins, and miscellaneous daggers, spears, breastplates, spurs, and sling bullets of lead and clay. Three of the ballista balls illustrated in Figure 5.10 came from Castillejo.

The other important camp was Fabius' headquarters, Peña Redonda. Schulten, out on one of his busman's-holiday Sunday reconnaissances with his devoted foreman, Juan Ibañez, found it

FIGURE 5.10
Soria, Museo Numantino, ballista balls from Numantia

easily. Its walls were visible, covered by only four to eight inches of topsoil overgrown with brush. And they also found a pick-head and a trowel which had been used in the building operations 2,039 years before. Schulten writes with infectious enthusiasm of these ground surveys, done at dawn or twilight to take advantage of the raking light which brings out the contours of the ancient walls, in a landscape redolent of thyme and rosemary, bright in the brief spring with poppies and anemones, the only sounds the hum of bees and the bleating of sheep passing through the *porta praetoria* to feed among the ruins of the barracks. He speaks warmly of the cooperation of the shepherds, glad to bring him their finds in exchange for a small tip or a photograph of themselves with their flocks. Schulten was so *simpático* that the archaeologist is always welcome in the neighborhood of Numantia and Renieblas, and there is a courteous expression of slight disappointment at the news that he is not German.

The thick cover of the *maquis* made it impossible to draw a plan without excavation. By request of the proprietor, the resulting walls were left uncovered; and, in 60 years, weather, men, and livestock have wrought much havoc. But, as Schulten found it, Peña Redonda was as well-preserved as Renieblas, and much the best-preserved of the camps around Numantia. It dominates the whole southern part of the town from a distance of little more than 500 yards; but it was also the most exposed of the camps, especially on the west and south, and here Fabius placed his artillery batteries (plan, Fig. 5.11) for different calibers of ball, some of which were found *in situ*. Schulten found two of the gates well-preserved. The *porta praetoria* on the north (Fig. 5.12) is 16 feet wide; its flanking towers made the camp wall 26 feet thick at these points. The east gate, 20 feet wide, had a protecting wall built in a curve in front of it. The *porta decumana* on the south, also 20 feet wide, opened into the main north-south camp street, the Via Praetoria, which was 50 feet wide. The main east-west street, the Via Principalis, is unique in its orientation: it is 100 feet wide, like the one at Renieblas, and here, as there, the military tribunes lived literally *in* this street, in comfortable quarters with patios. The street divides the camp into two unequal parts, two-thirds to the north, one-third to the south. The barracks were built of squared stone, by different work gangs, some of whom were better masons than others. Schulten made careful measurements to show that the camp was built on a system of modules dividing it into sixths, each 325 Roman feet

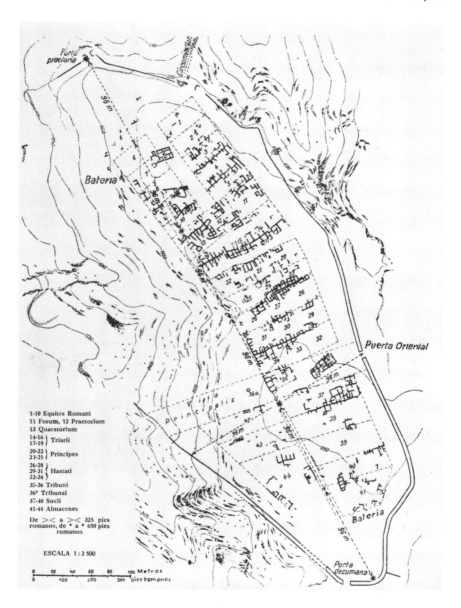

FIGURE 5.11
Numantia, Fabius's camp at Peña Redonda, plan

FIGURE 5.12
Peña Redonda, porta praetoria

long. The north and south sixths were drill grounds; the second sixth
(counting from the north) was for cavalry barracks; the third held
the headquarters (built Roman style, for Fabius bore an old Roman
name); the *quaestorium* for the supply officer, the forum with
booths for shops, and barracks for two-thirds of the infantry; the
fourth sixth held the rest of the infantry and the Via Principalis;
and the fifth sixth was reserved for the allied troops and the stores.
Schulten calculated that Fabius built his camp to hold 3,660 Romans
and 1,600 Italians, but that only half the strength was present at any
given time; here, as at Castillejo, the other half was held in reserve
or manned the circumvallation. The camp yielded the usual finds: one
remarkable one was a sherd stamped MAXI [mus] (for Fabius),
which Schulten thought was a ticket good for the issuing of ra-
tions.

Perseverance and discipline had built and manned these impressive
siege works; it now remained to starve Numantia out. The besieged
were 6,000 women and children and 4,000 men, hardly enough
to man the walls. For food they had their last harvest, plus 4,000
head of cattle without enough fodder to feed them. Their leader
was called Retogenes; the name is still used by the writer of a
protest column in the local Soria newspaper. One dark spring night

in 133 B.C., Retogenes, with four or five companions, and grooms with horses, made a last desperate attempt to break through Scipio's ring of steel and ride for help. They knifed the Roman guards at the Travesadas camp,, made it over the wall, horses and all, by the use of planks, and rode hell-for-leather to the nearest likely town, 33 miles away. The inhabitants agreed to help, but their elders betrayed the plan to Scipio, who galloped to the spot and had the hands of 400 able-bodied young men cut off. Things were now hopeless; famine after a nine-month siege left nothing to do but surrender.

The Numantines sent five envoys to ask honorable terms; Scipio insisted surrender should be unconditional. When the luckless envoys returned with the news, the townsfolk in a last paroxysm of Iberian pride murdered them. Famine reduced the Numantines first to eating animals, then to eating each other: first the dead, then the moribund, then the sick, then the feeble. Only when these had been consumed did they surrender. Many committed suicide. The rest were unkempt, with nails like claws, their clothes in rags. They reeked of pestilence; there was hate in their eyes. Scipio reserved 50 for his triumph in Rome and sold the rest into slavery. According to another tradition, the survivors all got drunk on beer, set fire to all their possessions, and then committed mass suicide, Retogenes first. However they died, their reputation was glorious: *parva civitas, sed gloria ingens*. On a state visit to Numantia, Alfonso XIII, invited to choose a souvenir, selected a little piece of charred wood from the Celtiberian town. Scipio himself survived his triumph by only three years. He died under mysterious circumstances in 129 B.C., a tragic figure, a would-be humanist involved in the brutality of war. As much as the heroism of Retogenes and his men, the memory of Scipio's presence and his victory consecrates the solitudes of Numantia.

The shell of the town survived, with traces of sparse habitation, and then came revival under Augustus. The town was now unwalled; as Tacitus was to write bitterly later, the Romans created a desert and called it peace: *solitudinem faciunt, pacem appellant*. The Romans kept the Celtiberian grid of streets, which they widened and drained. The new houses were better built, of dressed stone, with tile roofs, mosaics, frescoes, and little peristyles (Fig. 5.13). The town lasted, as a backwater, until the barbarian invasions of the fifth century A.D.; the evidence is coins, which end with Valentinian II

FIGURE 5.13
Numantia, Roman house

(A.D. 383–392). Its magistrates were Roman citizens, and we are told that it was famous for its pears. Today it lies deserted: quail dart from under the feet of the occasional visitor. It is best in March, when the wheat is green and the larks sing at dawning. There is often snow in late June, but soon after the grass is dry, the birds silent, the flowers withered, the eath hard, the river a trickle under the shimmering heat. Schulten writes eloquently of the drone of the reapers in August, the songs and dances. Then the swallows and the cranes fly south, the winter winds begin to blow. But still at sunset, over Scipio's camp at Castillejo, fly the eagles, symbol of the legions.

The fall of Numantia did not spell the end of the Celtiberian resistance. There was another uprising at the turn of the century. One of the Roman officers who served in it became, through the vicissitudes of Roman politics, himself a hero of the resistance movement. This was Sertorius, who, proscribed by the dictator Sulla, returned to Spain, learned to love the Spanish character and admire Spanish guerrilla tactics, set up a school to educate the sons of

Spanish noblemen, and fought (80–72 B.C.) for his adopted country against Pompey and other Roman generals until he was treacherously murdered in 72 B.C. Schulten's last two camps at Renieblas were set up against him by Pompey and his legate in 75/4 B.C. Camp IV was Pompey's summer headquarters, with walls and gates, but no stone barracks or artillery towers. Camp V was the legate's winter quarters; it has stone barracks, houses with dining rooms for colonels and staff, warehouses, artillery towers, and even 16 baths, along the north wall (the days of Scipionic austerity are over). Covering over 150 acres, it is the largest of all known Roman camps, and it is built on the flat: Sertorius may be dangerous, but the fear from Numantia is over.

Schulten discovered in 1910, and excavated from 1927 to 1930, what he identified as one of the camps built against Sertorius. This is Castra Caecilia, a little over a mile north of Cáceres, in Estremadura, in the far west of Spain. Its builder was Quintus Caecilius Metellus, proconsul in 79 B.C. The camp lies on a gentle slope, with a view (for military, not aesthetic purposes), on the Via de la Plata, which ran from the mines in the northwest to Hispalis (Seville); the modern main road to Placencia crosses its southeast corner. It is a rectangle (Fig. 5.14) measuring 2,200 by 1,300 Roman feet and enclosing a little over 50 acres—large enough for a legion. Its wall is the same thickness as that at Numantia—13 feet—and built in the same technique—stone facings with a rubble fill. Schulten found some of the camp streets indicated by field paths. Its orientation was based on sunrise in July, 79 B.C. It faced north, toward the enemy; its *praetorium* was of the same dimensions as the one at Castillejo, and, as there, was the type of a Greek peristyle house. It set the pattern for Imperial camps like Novaesium (Neuss) in Germany, and Lambaesis in Algeria. Its module, 650 Roman feet, is the same as Peña Redonda; it is a Greek surveyor's measure, the Olympic stade. The barrack size, too, is the same as at Peña Redonda. No weapons were found there: Schulten explained this by its having become a civilian colony, but some of his recent critics have argued that Schulten had camps on the brain, and found what he expected to find. The absence of weapons, the luxury, and the discovery of loom weights suggest to these critics that what Schulten found was not a camp but a civilian town. The probable solution is that it was first the one and then the other.

In his 1928 report, Schulten notes that he found no trace of buildings above ground; the remains, which lay only 18 inches below the surface, were much destroyed by the plow. In this campaign he excavated the forum, where he found shops stocked with lamps embossed with phallic symbols, and stone bases for the wooden columns of a temple with a lead roof (he found the melted remains) —the first ever discovered in a Roman camp; it probably belongs to the colonial phase. An altar to Serapis, found nearby, indicates the divinity worshiped there. The glassware and pottery, luxury items, Schulten explained as appropriate to a general's staff: Caecilius Metellus liked fine living.

In his final report (1930) Schulten featured the *praetorium*. Having found nothing in it, he deduced that the high command was spared by Sertorius and took their baggage; ordinary folk were not so lucky, hence the plethora of finds in the forum. He also reported on the *quaestorium*, where he found more evidence of luxury:

FIGURE 5.14
Castra Caecilia near Cáceres, plan

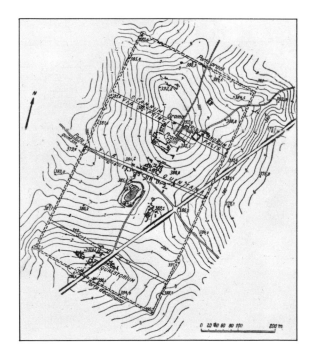

a bath. He found numerous coins, including some surprisingly old ones, of the third century B.C. (Was the site a native settlement before, as well as after, it was a camp?) He found some spurs, which his critics say are not Roman, and also some weapons: daggers, a ·saber, a round shield, and 31 ballista balls. Nineteen of these, however, had been put to a singularly pacific use: they were tastefully arranged as in a landscaped garden, with trees, at the southwest corner of the *praetorium*. He ends his report with a note on food and shelter; he found olive pits, the bones of the dog, pig, goat, deer, horse, and bull, and the charred remains of wood identified as olive and elm.

After the murder of Sertorius the Spanish resistance petered out. Caesar won some easy victories there as proquaestor in 69 B.C., and enriched Cádiz as well as himself. Twenty years later Spain was a battlefield in which Romans fought Romans. Caesar beat two Pompeian generals in 49 B.C. at Lérida, in the northeast; and in the spring of 45 B.C., Munda, south of Córdoba, was the scene of the final battle of the Civil War, in which the Pompeian remnant was liquidated. Spain was nearly ready for the blessings of the Augustan Peace.

6

FROM CAESAR
THROUGH NERVA

(44 B.C.-A.D. 98)

FIGURE 6.1

Madrid, Museo Arqueologico Nacional, bronze charter from Osuna (Lex Ursonis), detail. First seven lines require local magistrates to live within a mile of the town; Clause XCII concerns public embassies despatched by the colony.

IF WE ASK WHAT THE SPANIARDS GOT FROM the Romans to compensate for the loss of their independence, we find a ready answer in an archaeological discovery of the nineteenth century. This is the charter of the colony of Urso (Osuna [Seville]), an example of whose (Iberian) sculpture we have seen already (Fig. 4.13). The charter was inscribed in the first place on nine tablets of bronze, of which three were discovered in 1871 (part of one of them is illustrated in Fig. 6.1), and two more in 1875; from the letter styles, they are late first-century copies of the originals of 44 B.C. The great German epigraphists, Theodor Mommsen and Emil Hübner, made every effort to acquire them, but this time Spanish patriotism triumphed: their owner feigned a fever in order to evade the German emissaries, and the tablets are now on proud display in the Archaeological Museum in Madrid.

Urso was a center of Pompeian resistance to Julius Caesar in the Civil War which ended in 45 B.C.; the archaeological evidence is sling bullets, catapult balls—some of them conical, and of lead— and the towered walls, showing evidence of having been built by the defenders in a hurry. Once Caesar had won, he planned, and in 44 B.C. Mark Antony sent a colony of plebeians and freedmen from Rome to take over. The charter was thus conceived for and at first administered by Romans; but the Iberians benefited by the resulting law and order; and eventually, by intermarriage, native stock achieved status and Roman citizenship through officeholding.

123

It is worthwhile summarizing the contents of the charter, in order to show by a specific archaeological example precisely what is meant by the blessings of the Roman peace. Fifty-six detailed sections survive. Striking in the first place are the provisions for due process under Roman law. The first surviving section deals with judgments against debtors; there is a rubric on the collection of fines; and another on granting equal time to prosecutor and defendant in trials. The magistrates of the new colony, who had been nobodies in Rome, were now big frogs in a small puddle. Their prestige is protected as it would have been if they had been magistrates in Rome. They are escorted by lictors, and they have reserved seats in the circus and at the theater. The town council's decrees are binding on the magistrates, and it has the power to choose envoys from a panel submitted by the chief magistrates (*duumviri*). It must have been an expensive office, for an enormous fine is imposed on the man who fails either to go on the embassy or to provide an alternate. (This is the section reproduced in our photograph.)

The colony is a provincial copy of Rome. The town council sets the holidays, there are pontiffs and augurs as in the metropolis, and the same provision for expulsion from the council on moral grounds as was enforced against senators in Rome by the censors. Some actions are expressly forbidden: burial or cremation within the walls; operating a pottery or tile works of more than a certain capacity (to protect Italian industry?); unlawful assembly. The charter provides for public works such as paving and an aqueduct.

Especially noteworthy in the charter are provisions in the public interest. No building shall be demolished unless another is built in its place; the citizens' access to water is guaranteed; each public contractor must render an account of his stewardship to the town council within five months of finishing his job; clerks who handle money are bound to honesty by oath (one wonders if it worked); public land is inalienable; there is to be no carpetbagging—magistrates and council must be residents; and the council is empowered to investigate the magistrates at any time. Caesar obviously hoped to prevent in his colony the corruption which was rife in Rome; the *duumviri* are forbidden to accept gifts; they may not make gifts, or entertain lavishly (no more than nine guests at a time), while campaigning; and the council is forbidden to vote any reward for having held public office. No one connected with the founding of the colony, nor any relative of the founder, nor any Roman senator,

FIGURE 6.2

Tarragona, Roman wall with Iberian mason's marks. Note "Cyclopean" construction, lower left corner

may be adopted as its patron without a vote of three-quarters of the town council.

In return for all this paternalism, the colonists, resident aliens, and native Spaniards are liable to military service, and, between the ages of 14 and 60, to five days' *corvée* per year. Finally, the rights specified in the charter are guaranteed also to the colonists' wives. The document as a whole is an excellent example of an archaeological discovery illustrating the Roman legal mind at work; the Spaniards who lived under it must have considered that, on balance, they got their money's worth.

Caesar also gave colonial status to Tarragona, a city with an ideal climate and a prosperous hinterland, which since old Cato's time (195 B.C.) had been the capital of the Roman province of Hither Spain. The fill between the two faces of its handsome wall (Fig. 6.2) dates the fortification even earlier, to the time of P. Scipio (218 B.C.), for the sherds in it were found to be of the third century B.C. At the very bottom of the photograph may be seen the lower courses, built of huge, rough stones; it is what used to be called "Cyclopean"

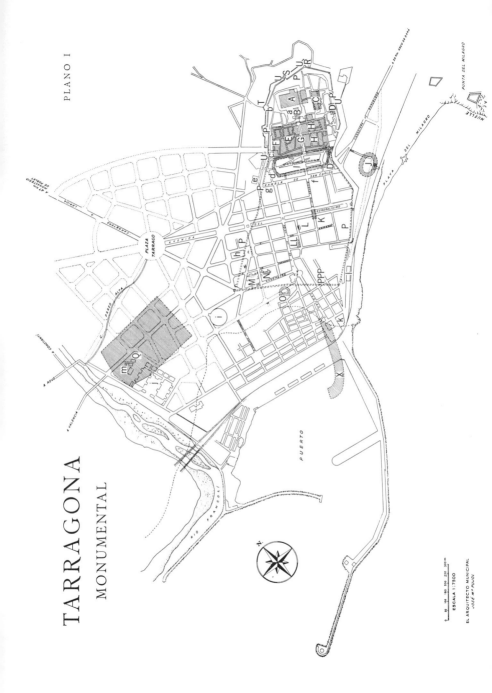

PLANO I

TARRAGONA
MONUMENTAL

FIGURE 6.3

Tarragona, plan

A. Remains of Roman camp (?)	LL. Temple of Minerva (?)	X. Mole of Roman port
B. Temple of Jupiter	M. Commercial forum	a. Cathedral
C. Temple of Augustus	N. Street and houses	b. Archepiscopal palace
D. Temple, dedicatee unknown	O. Theater	c. Audiencia
E. Forum	P. Roman walls	d. Ayuntamiento
F. Basilica	Q. Roman-Christian necropolis	e. Escuelas Saavedra
G. "Via Triumphalis"	R. Torre de San Magín	f. Barracks
H. Praetorium	S. Torre del Seminario	g. Instituto
I. Circus	T. Torre del Arzobisbo	h. Central market
J. Amphitheater	U. Gates	i. Bull ring
K. Temple, dedicatee unknown	V. Roman quay	j. Tobacco factory
L. Remains of arches		k. Port authority
		l. Railway station
		m. Necropolis Museum

work, and it used to be dated as early as the sixth century before Christ. But recently walls of the same type in Italy—at Alba Fucens and Cosa, for example *—have been dated in the third century B.C., and so the lower courses at Tarragona are probably not earlier than Scipio. The upper courses, whose squared and trimmed ("rusticated") blocks are of Roman dimensions (one and a half by three Roman feet) must have been built to Roman order—perhaps Cato's—by Iberian masons, for, as the photograph shows, they bear Iberian masons' marks.

Tarragona was built on three terraces, and the surviving stretch of early wall embraces two of these (see plan, Fig. 6.3). Here the remains are of much later date; coins, and the style of the architectural fragments, date them to the time of Augustus, who was in Tarragona in 25 B.C. recuperating from a serious illness contracted in the Cantabrian campaign in the northwest. It was he who gave the colony its full resounding title: *Colonia Julia Victrix Triumphalis Tarraco*. On the middle terrace may still be seen the remains of a 50-foot tower of the huge headquarters where he lay convalescing—called

---

* See *The Mute Stones Speak*, pp. 95 ff.

Torre de Pilatos because the procurator of Judaea was supposed once to have dwelt in it as Roman governor of Spain. The underground chamber beneath the vaulted hall within makes it more likely that the tower served as a prison. Its present ruinous state is due to an attempt by the French to blow it up in 1813. The Via Triumphalis, nowadays the Calle Mayor, divides the headquarters building from the paved forum to the north. Figure 6.4 shows an Augustan gate into the forum.

On the upper terrace, under the cathedral, lie the remains of the once-lofty temple of Jupiter, not the Roman but the Egyptian god, Jupiter Ammon, portrayed with ram's horns. Augustus may have chosen this aspect of the Father of Gods and Men on account of his desire to be compared with Alexander the Great, whom the Egyptian god had saluted as a world conqueror over 300 years before on an oasis in the Western Desert. A huge stone medallion, four feet across, with a relief of Jupiter Ammon, was found on the site. Also on the upper terrace may have been the barracks of a legion, as well as a temple of Augustus himself; outside of Italy, he allowed himself to be worshiped as a god. The Spanish professor Quintilian records how the citizens of Tarragona reported with glee to Augustus that a palm tree had miraculously sprouted on the altar of his temple. "Aha!" said the fearsome Emperor, "That proves how long you take between sacrifices to me."

The lower terrace was entirely taken up with the circus, where verse inscriptions were found celebrating the victories of charioteers; one is promised—in Greek—eternal memory in the chatter over his wins. Vaults in house basements indicate where the shops in its fabric once were; it, too, suffered from French explosives in 1813. South of the circus, nearer the sea, work is in progress detaching from the fabric of a church the amphitheater, for gladiatorial contests, as large as the better-preserved one in Nîmes and with a magnificent view of the sea. The building of the railway line partly destroyed it. Augustus, or his governor, from the headquarters building above, could look down into the circus or the amphitheater without having to attend. One end is cut in the rock; the spalls from it were used to build up the lower end. West of the amphitheater was the harbor, which cut farther into the land than today; archaeologists have found traces of its mole. Schulten records with indignation how, in executing harbor works in 1906, a myriad of ancient statues, reliefs, friezes, mosaics, amphoras, and coins were wantonly thrown into the sea.

The area west of the circus belongs to a post-Augustan expansion of the town; it includes a commercial forum, with shops, and the sorry remains of a theater, buried beneath an oil factory. The necropolis, of very late date (third to sixth century A.D.), was found in 1923 beneath the tobacco factory. The most touching find from it, now in the local museum, is a jointed ivory doll, found in the grave of a six-year-old girl who had been buried in a gold-bordered tunic.

The most impressive Roman site in Spain is Mérida (Badajoz). Founded in 25 B.C. by Augustus' lieutenant Agrippa for time-expired

FIGURE 6.4
Tarragona, forum arch

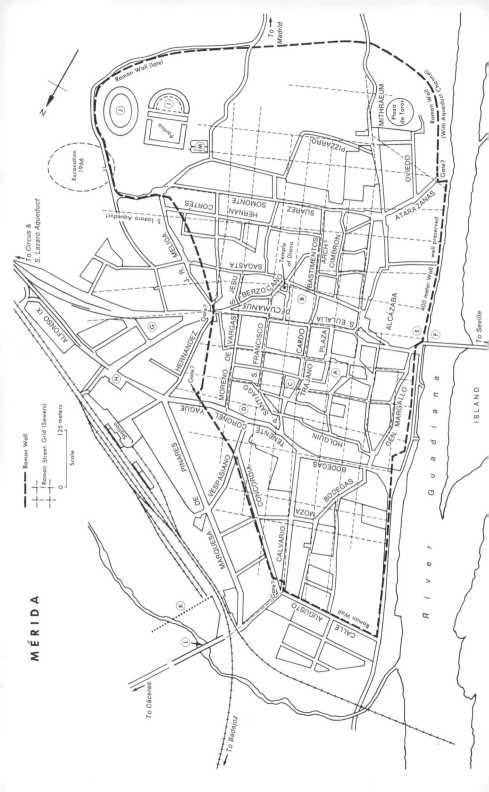

MÉRIDA

veterans (in Latin, *emeriti;* its Roman name was Augusta Emerita), it became the capital of the province of Lusitania, and prospered to the point where the Gallic poet Ausonius, writing in the fourth century A.D., could rank it as the ninth city in the Empire, after Rome, Constantinople, and Alexandria, but before Athens. It has been well-nicknamed "the Rome of Spain." Among its almost inexhaustible variety of Roman monuments are included (see plan, Fig. 6.5) two bridges, a river port, two reservoirs, three aqueducts, walls, drains, temples, a theater, an amphitheater, a circus, luxurious private houses, commemorative monuments, over 200 inscriptions, and some 70 pieces of sculpture. Its chief excavator was José Ramon Mélida, whose archaeological experience had been gained at Numantia, which he took over from Schulten; at Mérida the modern town fathers have expressed their gratitude by naming after Mélida the street that leads from the amphitheater he excavated to the main part of the town.

The best approach to Mérida is across the handsome Guadiana River bridge (Fig. 6.6), over 2,500 feet long and supported by 60 arches. Agrippa's engineers supplied in addition relieving-arches and breakwater piers pointing upstream to reduce the pressure of the river in flood. Yet floods and the even more terrible hand of man have necessitated repeated restorations, sometimes using stone from other Roman monuments. The English and their Spanish allies cut the bridge in 1811 to deny it to the French. Since 1912 it has been a national monument, which, it is to be hoped, will spare it further depredations.

The Romans, being famous hydraulic engineers, took great pains with Mérida's water supply. The local name for its reservoir, something over three miles to the northwest, is Pantano de Proserpina (Fig. 6.7). It was named from an inscription found nearby, which has nothing to do with the reservoir but invokes the curse of the goddess

FIGURE 6.5

Mérida, plan

A. Museum	G. Santa Eulalia monument
B. Temple of Jupiter (Capitolium)	H. Temple of Mars
C. Arch "of Trajan"	I. Theater
D. Temple of Concord, now Parador	J. Amphitheater
E. Alcazaba	K. Los Milagros aqueduct
F. Bridge	L. Bridge
M. Casa basilica	

FIGURE 6.6
Mérida, Guadiana bridge

on a clothes-robber. The massive masonry dike, granite-revetted, is 1,385 feet long, from 7 to 11½ feet thick, and 30 feet high; it holds 10,000,000 cubic meters of water, unfortunately no longer potable.

The reservoir supplied the longest and most impressive of Mérida's aqueducts, called from its massive arches Los Milagros, "The Miracles" (Fig. 6.8). The nomenclature is not without humor, however; a fat pentagonal pillar at a turn is called Milagro Gordo, "The Fat Miracle." Of its original length of over seven miles, just over half a mile survives, on 37 buttressed piers, with three stories of arches, reaching a total height of over 80 feet. The piers have a cement core, revetted alternately with granite and with brick, five courses each. The resulting white and red pattern pleased the Moors, who imitated it in the color scheme of the arches in their great mosque in Córdoba.

Agrippa's Mérida was a square, like a Roman camp, or like
Augusta Praetoria (Aosta) in north Italy, which was founded about
the same time. Four hundred meters of its wall are preserved to the
east of the bridge; a two-arched gate on the north, very like the Porta
Marina at Pompeii, has been excavated—it was the symbol of the
town, appearing on its coins. On the west, the remains of the "Arco
de Trajano" are really Augustan and mark the exit through the
original wall of the main north-south street, the *cardo*; later, perhaps
under Trajan and Hadrian—the Spanish emperors—the walls were
extended, doubling the size of the town. The main east-west street,
the *decumanus*, ran from the bridge; the bridgehead gate now forms
part of a garage. The grid of the Roman streets is revealed by the
ancient drains which turn up every time excavations are made for a
new building.

FIGURE 6.7
Mérida, Pantano de Proserpina reservoir

FIGURE 6.8
Mérida, Los Milagros aqueduct

One way or another, four of Mérida's temples are more or less well-preserved. In the sixteenth century, the Conde de los Corbos built his house around the Temple "of Diana" (probably in fact the Temple of Rome and Augustus). The result was the preservation of several of its fluted granite columns with Corinthian capitals; it closely resembled the nearly contemporary Maison Carrée at Nîmes. The violet Corinthian columns of the Temple of Mars, outside the walls, were cut down and reused in a shrine of Eulalia, the city's partonsaint. An inscription reads IAM NON MARTI SED IESV CHRISTO DOMINO. The entablature survives, with alternating palmettes and Gorgon's heads in relief; a section of the architrave was used as a step, the trophies with which it was engraved set face outward. Acanthus leaves were the motif of the cornice. The dedication to Mars is guaranteed by an inscription of Neronian date, recording the consecration by a rich woman to the god in memory of her husband. The Temple of Concord lies under a building which was once a convent, afterward a prison, now a charming government hotel. Its altar, inscribed CONCORDIAE AVGVSTAE, was preserved through having been one of three superimposed in the seventeenth century and used as a pedestal for a statue of St. Eulalia (Fig. 6.9). The altars are decorated with swags, ribbons, ox skulls, the peaked cap of a *flamen* (priest), and the sacrificial ax and saucer. The bottom altar of the three is unfinished; it had been waiting for an order in the stonecutter's yard. To the south, by the bull ring and the river, inscriptions and a statue, which once had

FIGURE 6.9
Mérida, St. Eulalia monument

FIGURE 6.10

Mérida, air view of northeast quarter, showing circus, amphitheater, and theater

eyes inset in a gleaming material, revealed the presence of a temple to the Oriental divinities Serapis and Mithra, beloved of sailors and soldiers; we must not forget that Mérida was a river port, and, as a provincial capital, the headquarters of a legion.

Reconstruction has made the theater Mérida's most impressive surviving monument. The aerial photograph (Fig. 6.10) shows its location on the outskirts of the town and its relation to the amphitheater and the circus. When Mélida began to excavate it in 1910, from the earth projected only seven piers, regarded by the inhabitants as the thrones of seven Moorish kings who had once, they thought, sat there to deliberate the fate of the city. In the eighteenth century it was a bull ring. Thereafter, forgotten, disfigured, ruined, earth-covered, it degenerated into a chick-pea patch. An early excavation photograph (Fig. 6.11) shows the amount of earth Mélida had to remove to get down to the level of the orchestra and stage building. Its final destruction was wrought by an earthquake: Mélida found a skeleton crushed between two columns. An inscription over one entrance arch (it can be seen lying across the entrance in Figure 6.11) records its building by Agrippa in his third consulship, which fell in 27 B.C.

Mélida's excavation exceeded all his expectations, bringing to light a luxury unusual in a provincial theater: vast quantities of marbles, columns, bases, capitals, cornices, friezes, statues, pedestals, and inscriptions. One inscription, recording that each spectator was alloted the equivalent of 22 inches of space, enabled him to calculate the theater's capacity: it was 5,500. The best seats were reserved for the "knights," the rest for the plebs. They had separate entrances and no intercommunication. This class distinction was one of the dubious blessings of the Roman peace. The theater was cut into a hillside, making for excellent acoustics. The orchestra was paved with alternate squares of blue and white marble. The riser at the front of the stage was embellished with alternate rectangular and semicircular niches, with blue and white marble moldings, and steps at the ends. The stage itself was long and narrow in the usual Roman fashion: 200 by 26 feet. In it Mélida found 12 put-holes, with nails and fragments of wood in the bottom. The holes may have held masts for awnings

FIGURE 6.11
Mérida, theater, early stage of excavation

to shade the best seats, or they may have had something to do either with the curtain—which in an ancient theater was always lowered, not raised, at the beginning of a performance—or with stage sets.

The richly baroque stage building (Fig. 6.12) which Mélida largely re-erected (from 2,700 fragments of architectural members) is too ornate for Augustan taste; it is probably Hadrianic (A.D. 117–138), perhaps restored after a fire. It has two stories and three doors, turning in bronze-lined pivot-holes, with columned niches for statues on either side. The dado was of violet marble, the shafts of the columns of polished unfluted blue, with white bases and capitals, which were probably gilded. The back wall of the niches was brick, stuccoed with red, and with pilasters to break the surface, corresponding to the columns. The central door was set at the back of a hemicycle and roofed with a coffered half-dome. Over the central door was a statue of Augustus; the niches contained statues of Trajan, Hadrian, Pluto, Proserpina, Venus, Ceres, Minerva, and Jupiter. Backstage were six green-rooms for the actors, with built-in benches, and, in one, a table. Their ceilings were supported by granite columns stuccoed red and ocher. Behind the stage building Mélida's successor A. Floriano in 1934–1936 excavated a portico 150 feet wide, for shelter in case of rain. It was paved with polychrome mosaic, and the garden it enclosed had two semicircular benches (*exedrae*). This rather overwhelming décor compares for richness with any to be found anywhere in the Empire.

Fifty feet to the east of the theater lies the amphitheater; in the drain between was found a colossal marble hand which may have belonged to a statue of Augustus. The amphitheater is of average size, smaller than the one at Italica, larger than the ones at Paestum and Ventimiglia in Italy. It had 33 rows of seats; if spectators sat as close as in the theater, it would have held between 14,000 and 15,000. An inscription on the granite balustrade of the judges' tribunal (Fig. 6.13) dates the building to the year in which Augustus held the tribunician power for the sixteenth time; this was 8 B.C. The construction is much more economical than that of the theater. The cement core is faced partly with brick, and the outer face is in ·no way monumentalized. There is no way of telling how ornate the north entrance arch was, for it was badly damaged in modern times by contractors using explosives to get building materials. It had 16 entrances, each flanked by a pair of stairs; there was no distinction of classes and masses as in the theater. The earth from the excavation

FIGURE 6.12
Mérida, theater, stage building

FIGURE 6.13
Mérida, amphitheater, judges' tribunal, with inscription of 8 B.C.

of the arena was used by the original builders as fill on which to erect
the seats. For safety the arena lies a good two meters below the lowest
row of seats. Besides its north and south entrances, with their chariot
ruts, are small rooms (with latrines adjacent) where gladiators awaited
their turn. In the center of the arena is a deep pit approached by five
parallel corridors; these will have been for the beasts, which may have
been raised to the arena by elevators, as in the Coliseum in Rome; *

---

* See *The Mute Stones Speak*, pp. 233–235 and Fig. 9.6.

the excavators found settings for gratings through which the beasts were fed. The pit also allowed space for sets representing forests, mythological scenes, and the like, against which the beast fights were staged.

Excavation of Mérida's circus, a quarter-mile beyond the late extension of the city wall to the east, began in 1920. It is two-thirds the length of the Circus Maximus in Rome. The *spina*, around which the charioteers made their laps, runs obliquely to allow a wider space at the start; its ends are curved to reduce danger from accidents; upon it were set statues and egg-shaped counters which were taken down one by one as the laps were run. The stands would seat 26,000 to 30,000. If Mélida found any criteria for dating, he does not report it; but the circus was still a going concern in the fourth century A.D. An inscription records repairs in the reigns of the sons of Constantine (A.D. 337–340).

Mosaics from a number of private houses are on display in the Alcázaba (the Moorish castle over the Roman port installations southeast of the bridge), the theater, and the local museum. The most impressive mosaic—in the Alcázaba—was discovered in 1834 in the process of digging a well. It has a pronounced literary flavor: in the central medallion are actors with mask, staff, and lyre; adjoining are eight of the nine muses; on one side of the surround, Apollo with the winged horse Pegasus, symbolizing poetic inspiration. Scenes from the conventional mosaic pattern-book fill out the field: in the corners, the four seasons; and on the other three sides of the surround, Nile scenes whose inspiration comes from Alexandria:—river navigation, pygmies dancing.

By the west wall of the portico behind the theater lies the Casa basilica, a Roman luxury dwelling apparently converted to Christian uses, for one of the rooms contains, as a late addition, a rectangular tank suitable for use in baptism by total immersion. A painting of a dove in a medallion may be a Christian symbol. The occasion for the conversion may have been the martyrdom of St. Eulalia (A.D. 303/304). The house has painted, windowed apses surmounted by half-domes; the dados are painted to imitate marble; the style shows architectural perspective as in the Pompeian second style, which was fashionable in the time of Augustus; this gives a possible date for an early phase of the house. Figures in the apse wear gold ornaments and sandals studded with painted emeralds; their white tunics,

FIGURE 6.14

Mérida, grave-relief of inn-keeper drawing wine from a barrel

bordered with purple and gold, stand out boldly against a background of Pompeian red.

One hundred yards farther east is the "Casa del anfiteatro," recently excavated—with the use of a bulldozer!—and restored. In the restoration, the mosaics were taken up, backed with crinoline and glue, and replaced on new cement foundations. Little pitched roofs now protect the tops of the surviving walls; some stuccoed granite columns have been re-erected in the peristyle; trees have been planted. Though dating by stratification has proved impossible—the site was used as a dump for the excavations of theater and amphitheater—the excavators report pottery and lamps of the late first century found under the floors. The prize mosaic comes from what was probably the dining room. It is an autumn scene (late second- early third centuries A.D.) with three lively figures holding hands and treading grapes in a vat. The dating is based on a similarity in style with the mosaics, especially those of the House of the Labors of Hercules in the wealthy northeast quarter of Volubilis in Morocco, whose proprietors flourished under the Severan dynasty (A.D. 193–235).

FIGURE 6.15
Mérida, head of Augustus

Of the finds in the local museum we illustrate two. In an inscription with late and barbarous spelling (Fig. 6.14) a man who was probably a tavern keeper commemorates his dead wife, with whom he lived for 16 years. The accompanying relief shows him drawing wine into a pitcher from a barrel resting on sawhorses. A fine head of Augustus (Fig. 6.15) shows him wearing his hair in his favorite style (that of Alexander the Great); his head is veiled for sacrifices. It is appropriate that we should end our account of Mérida as we began it, with Augustus; because, though it lasted long after his time, it was essentially his foundation, designed to symbolize, as it still does, the might and majesty of Imperial Rome.

Another evidence of Roman Imperial majesty is the aqueduct of Segovia, whose date is controversial but may well be Augustan. The town, capital of the province of the same name, lies only 60 miles northwest of Madrid. A resistance center, it was the scene of a Roman defeat of the Sertorians in 75 B.C.; yet 50 years later, if its aqueduct is Augustan, it was enjoying the amenities of the

FIGURE 6.16
Segovia, aqueduct

Roman peace—as it still does, for the aqueduct is in working order. Its 128 surviving arches run for half a mile, on two levels, rising at the highest point, in the very center of the town (Fig. 6.16), over 90 feet above street level. It is built of granite, the blocks set without mortar. The arches are so high that their massiveness seems delicate. The Segovians have placed a likeness of the monument on their coat of arms, though the Roman Hercules on the highest pier was replaced in the sixteenth century by the Madonna and St. Sebastian; but it is the sense of pagan Roman hugeness that still dominates the city.

The next finds to be discussed are Spanish in interest and probably Augustan in date, though they were discovered in Italy and are now in the Terme museum in Rome. These are the four silver cups (Fig. 6.17) found in 1857 at Aquae Apollinares (Vicus Aurelii, nowadays Vicarello) on the north shore of the Lago di Bracciano, 30 miles northwest of Rome. Engraved on the cups is the itinerary of a journey from Cádiz to Rome, with the names of 45 staging points (*mansiones*) within Spain. On the cup farthest left can be seen the names of the stopping places along the Via Augusta from Valentia to the border. The most important (see map, Fig. 6.18) are Valentia, Saguntum, Dertosa (an Augustan colony, nowadays Tortosa), Tarraco, Gerunda (Gerona), and Iuncaria (Junquera, still the customs boundary between France and Spain on the Le Perthus route). In its earlier stages, the route circles Cádiz Bay to Portus Menesthei (Puerto de Santa Maria), then strikes northward to Hasta Regia (Jerez de la Frontera) and Hispalis (Seville). Then it turns northeastward and follows the Guadiana River through Carmo (Carmona), Astigi (an Augustan colony, nowadays Écija), to Corduba, birthplace of the philosopher and tragic poet Seneca. On the next stretch it passes through Epora (Montoro), Castulo (Cazlona, near Linares), Libisosa (an Augustan colony, nowadays Lezuza), Saltigi (Chinchilla de Monte Aragon), and Saetibis (Játiva), to link up with the Via Augusta at Valentia. On this last stretch it passes through the country where Iberian culture was strongest: Balazote and Cerro de los Santos are not far out of the way.

FIGURE 6.17
Rome, Terme,
Vicarello cups

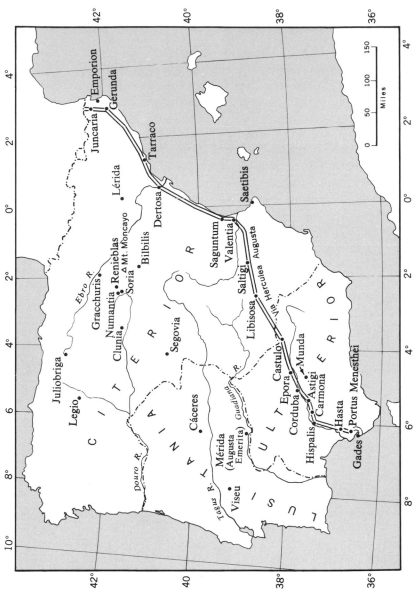

FIGURE 6.18
*Spain,
133 B.C.–A.D. 96,
to illustrate
Chapters 5
and 6*

The cups look like milestones, and are meant to. Augustus was much interested in the road network: Agrippa made a road map of the Empire; a milestone appears on the coins of L. Vinucius, about 16 B.C., who was responsible for the resurfacing of the Via Flaminia from Rome to Rimini; and from about 20 B.C. dates the Milliarium Aureum (Golden Milestone), a gilt-bronze column in the forum at Rome marking the starting point of all the main roads from Rome and bearing the names of the chief cities of the Empire, with their distances from Rome. It is a reasonable conjecture that the Vicarello cups are a by-product of this Augustan interest in land communications.

The next site to be described is significant not in itself, but as an example of how Augustus pacified northwest Spain after the Cantabrian War of 29–19 B.C. This is Julióbriga (Santander), at the headwaters of the Ebro. The Cantabrians, like the Numantines, thought liberty worth more than Latin and made the Romans pay dear for their victory. Mothers killed their sons rather than have them fall into Roman hands. A boy with a stolen sword killed his father and brother in prison at his father's order and then burned himself alive. The Cantabrians sang their victory song as the Romans nailed them on the cross. To cheat the Romans of a triumph, they scorched their earth, slit their throats, or took poison. When the Romans enslaved them, they would kill their masters and return home. No wonder Agrippa's soldiers mutinied rather than fight them. But after ten long years they were finally pacified and dragged, recalcitrant every step of the way, into what the Romans regarded as civilization. They soon found service as mercenaries in the Roman army. Men from Julióbriga served on the Nile, on the Danube, in Britain; there is a tombstone of one of them in Numidia, and another in Mainz. Julióbriga is an example of what Romanization meant: a Roman town in the plain, wherein Cantabrians, forced down from their hilltop fastnesses, formed the lower classes and learned to do their duty.

Figure 6.19 shows excavation in progress at Julióbriga. In the middle distance, near the village church of Reinosa, a crew is excavating a luxurious building of some importance, with mosaic floors and red stucco walls, like the House of the Vettii in Pompeii; some of its columns were Tuscan (plain), others spiral-fluted. The finds included amber, jewelry, fine pottery, and coins ranging in date from 20 B.C.

FIGURE 6.19
Julióbriga (Santander), excavation in progress

to the reign of Caracalla (A.D. 211–217). In the foreground another villa is being excavated. The archaeologist in charge reports that it took forty men a month to move 470 cubic meters of earth. The building is a villa with a portico originally supported on pilasters; behind the portico, 26 rooms arranged around a peristyle. This in itself is not remarkable; there are dozens of villas like it in Spain and Portugal. But what *is* remarkable is that here at last it is possible to date the building by the pottery. This was not done by the original excavator (who published under a pseudonym) but by the accurate and unflagging Maria Angeles Mesquiriz de Catalan, who in 1961 published a two-volume work in which at last some attempt was made to date the embossed ware (*terra sigillata*) found on sites like this one. The pottery bears makers' marks that match those found on accurately dated sites in South Gaul. Thus the mark OF PAT, found here, has a "horizon of the second half of the first century A.D.," and the villa was in its prime from A.D. 35 to 75. Coins show it existed earlier and went on being inhabited later; they range in date from Mark Antony (who committed suicide in 30 B.C) to Caracalla.

Bilbilis, in iron-mining country on a hilltop three miles northeast of Calatayud (Zaragoza) deserves brief mention here because it was the birthplace, about A.D. 40, of the epigrammatic poet Martial. Like many another Spaniard—the Senecas, Lucan, Quintilian—he left Spain for Rome to seek his fortune; but, unlike them, he came home again, for he did not prosper in the metropolis. There for 30 years he had suffered toil, envy, want, the patron, and almost the jail, thinking it worth it (it was like Paris in the '20s or Vienna in the '90s) for it was the capital of the world'with its splendid imperial court, its rich houses, its amusements, colonnades, piazzas, and parks. He plumbed the life of the metropolis to the very depths; but when a rich patron, the letter writer Pliny the Younger, offered to pay Martial's way back to Spain and a rich patroness named Marcella gave him a small farm near his birthplace, he was glad enough to accept, being by now faint of heart and light of purse. The poems he wrote about his last half-dozen years of the simple life in Bilbilis cast a golden glow over middle class existence in rural Spain in the first century A.D. This was the Roman peace at its best: a grove and a spring, a vineyard and a rose garden, a fishpond and a dovecote, and an old woman to wait on him. Oak logs burned on his hearth; good things bubbled in pots; a friendly hunter provided game; his bailiff managed his handful of slaves. Here, as never in Rome, he could throw his toga aside and sleep.

Bilbilis bears an Iberian name. It is a typical Romanized Iberian hill town, at the confluence of two rivers, with houses picturesquely perched on terraces. The path to it winds up a ravine to the forum, between two temple-crowned hills; nowadays the temples have become the hermitages of Santa Barbara and San Paterno, the latter looking down into a deep gorge. From the terrace of the other temple, and from the rock-cut theater beside it, there is a magnificent view at sunset, to gilded saw-toothed mountains under a lavender sky. We can imagine Martial enjoying the view and hearing the familiar sounds he had missed so much in the midst of the hurly-burly of Rome: the chirp of crickets, the chunk of mattocks, the hiss of the hot steel dipped by the smith in the river to temper the famous Celtiberian swords. Martial's homesickness for these simple Spanish things is the most admirable thing about him.

Clunia Sulpicia, nowadays Coruña del Conde (Burgos), fits into the chronology at A.D. 68 because in that year the Roman general Galba, a pretender to the throne, was there when he heard the news of

Nero's suicide. It was a strategic road junction and readily defensible, since its walls follow a line of sheer cliffs all around. It was a center of resistance under Sertorius in 75 B.C. Under the Romans it was a double city, for Celtiberians and colonists, and so its area is enormous: over 320 acres—bigger than Mérida at its greatest extent and over five times the area of Tarragona. The excavations revealed the forum, a theater with a three-story stage building, a sumptuous villa, and a potter's shop with a complete stock of vases of all shapes and sizes, a coin and two inscriptions of Galba, and an amusing inscription in which a hunter boasts in bad verse of his prowess at killing wild boars and stags.

To the age of Domitian (A.D. 81–96) belong the most sumptuous painted tombs in the vast necropolis near Carmona, 20 miles east of Seville. The excavation (1881–1915) was due to a local pharmacist, J. Fernández Lopez, and the artist son of a Nottingham industrialist, George Bonsor. The site contains over 900 family tombs; most were cremation burials. In the richer graves a glass urn is inclosed in a lead box within a stone container in a masonry chamber deep in the earth, reached by rock-cut steps, and closed by a stone so heavy it would take several men to lift it. Libation tubes made possible liquid offerings to the dead; there were also offered vases in clay and glass, bottles just big enough to hold a single tear, rings, coins, fibulae, ivory, ostrich eggs, bone pins, and mirrors. Infants were buried in amphoras, not cremated. The richest tombs are stuccoed and painted. The Tomb of the Funeral Banquet (Fig. 6.20) portrays a group of banqueters playing musical instruments; from one side a latecomer approaches, from the other a servant with platters of food. Several of

FIGURE 6.20

Carmona, Tomb of the Funeral Banquet, watercolor of fresco

the tombs have three-dimensional banqueting chambers. The Tomb of the Columbarium-Triclinium has three couches cut in the rock, a footbath, and a kitchen; the Tomb of the Elephant—so called from a stone elephant, probably Iberian, found in one of its rooms—has no less than three banquet rooms: one for summer, open to the sky; one for winter, shaded with a trellis; and one underground. There is a seat for the slave butler at the right of the entrance stair, a bath, a cloakroom, a pantry, a kitchen with chimney, and a burial chamber with niches for six urns. The Tomb of the Servilii has an atrium surrounded by two stories of columns and roofed with an oval cupola; trapezoidal chambers open off. There is an exotic air about the necropolis. Some of the architectural forms are Greek; some of the offerings Punic; and the elephant, as we saw, probably Iberian. (The Romans were perfectly willing to let native customs and culture survive as long as their subjects behaved.)

This chapter has surveyed a small sample of the rich archaeological evidence of what the Roman peace meant to Spain. The charter of Urso exemplifies Roman law and order; Tarragona and Mérida are two provincial capitals, one austere, the other flamboyant. The Segovia aqueduct and the itinerary on the Vicarello cups offer examples of the material amenities, in water supply and well-kept roads, which the Romans offered as compensation to the people they conquered. Julióbriga, that city of the plain whose townsfolk, once hostile, did far-flung service in the Roman army; and Bilbilis, that city of the hills where one who had tasted the fleshpots of Rome delighted in rural retirement, give the flavor of life in the smaller towns. In sprawling Clunia, Roman and native lived side by side. The Roman had his villa, the native had the delights of a Roman theater nearly as big as Mérida's. And in Carmona we have the evidence that Imperial Rome did not disturb, in death any more than in life, the pious observances of her loyal subjects. Spain prospered in the first century of the Empire; in the next generation, under Emperors born on her own soil, she was to prosper even more.

7

SPAIN UNDER THE
SPANISH EMPERORS

(A.D. 98-138)

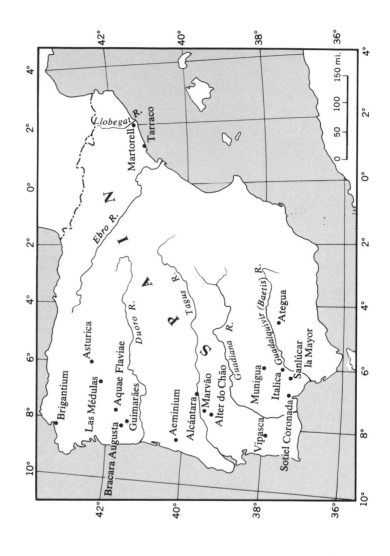

FIGURE 7.1
*Iberian Peninsula
under Trajan
and Hadrian*

U̲NDER ITS SPANISH-BORN EMPERORS, TRAJAN (A.D. 98–117) and Hadrian (A.D. 117–138), the Iberian peninsula blossomed with splendid new architecture in sanctuaries, towns, and provincial capitals; with ambitious public works: roads, aqueducts, bridges, and lighthouses. The prosperity was largely due to the successful exploitation of Iberian mines. The archaeological evidence for the golden age of material well-being will be the subject of this chapter.

German and Spanish archaeologists in collaboration have been excavating since 1956 one of the most remarkable examples of Roman architectural skill in Spain: the terraced sanctuary at Mulva (ancient Munigua), in the almost inaccessible foothills of the Sierra Morena, 36 miles north of Seville (see map, Fig. 7.1). The terraces rise on three levels (Fig. 7.2). On the lowest (lower right in the photograph, in front of the buttresses) was the forum, with a portico, temple, and town offices. In the latter the Germans discovered a treasure: a complete bronze inscription (Fig. 7.3), which incidentally proves that Munigua flourished before the Trajanic date to which they assign the sanctuary above. The inscription is a letter from the Emperor Titus (A.D. 79–81), precisely dated, on the seventh of September, A.D. 79 (about two weeks after Vesuvius destroyed Pompeii), to the *quattuorviri* (mayors) and town council, forgiving them a debt of

FIGURE 7.2
Munigua, terraced sanctuary

500,000 sesterces ($25,000 uninflated) in view of the allegedly strapped condition of the town finances.

Near the forum were the baths. At the bottom of the *frigidarium* was found a handsome head of a girl with a page-boy bob (Fig. 7.4). The excavators have named her "Hispania." They think of her as the type of a Roman province personified, a common motif in Hadrianic art. Her stylized beauty owes something to the Iberian tradition, and she, like the sanctuary as a whole, provides proof that culture at this time in Spain maintained a high level even in remote places.

The terraces at Munigua are of great interest, not only because they are unique in Spain (those at Tarragona are much less spectacular and symmetrical), but also because they echo so exactly the terraces of the Sanctuary of Fortuna at Praeneste in Italy, built by Sulla about

FIGURE 7.3
Munigua, bronze inscription, letter of Titus

FIGURE 7.4 *Munigua, "Hispania"*

80 B.C.* The finds date the Munigua terrace in the late first or early second century A.D. The terrace faces east, toward the city. It is axially symmetrical, planned on the module of the Roman foot of 30 centimeters. The center of the axis is the point of convergence of the two ramps (Fig. 7.5) which lead from the second, or town terrace, to the temple at the top. As at Praeneste, the visitor's vision is forced upward, and the climax is heightened by heightened color. The excavators found several thousand fragments of marble veneer. They discovered that the architects used more color as they built upward, from white and gray at the bottom to 15 different colors of marble at the top, used on walls, cornices, and capitals of the most flamboyant order, the composite, combining Corinthian acanthus leaves with Ionic volutes.

The ramps lead to a platform from which lateral stairs rise at the north and south ends to the temple level. The semicircle of an exedra cuts deeply into the forecourt of the temple. The architect borrowed this feature from the Temple of Hercules Victor at Tivoli,† near Rome, which may be by the same hand as the Praeneste sanctuary. The exedra is surrounded on three sides by high walls, making a court, with engaged columns and shallow niches. The entrance to the temple is in the center of the back (west) wall of the court.

The temple precinct was surrounded by a raised, U-shaped portico, accessible by shallow flights of steps. At the back of the open space between temple and portico are put-holes, which probably once held flower pots. The temple terrace is heavily buttressed at the back. Attached on the northwest is a series of rooms for the sacristans and the temple gear. They are built on caissons filled with gravel, a feature noted also at Praeneste. The deity worshiped in the temple is unknown; because of the likenesses in architecture to Praeneste and Tivoli, the excavators suggest as candidates either Fortuna Augusta or Hercules of Cádiz. Mineral wealth built the sanctuary, and when the mines were worked out, in the third or fourth century A.D., it gradually fell into disrepair.

The director of the Munigua excavation has been called away to administrative duties in West Berlin, which will delay further work

---

* See *The Mute Stones Speak*, pp. 116–130.
† *Ibid.*, p. 136, Fig. 5.10.

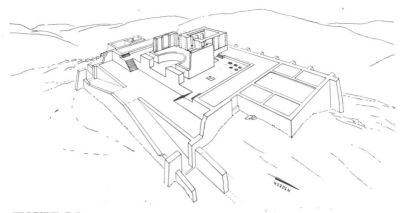

FIGURE 7.5
Munigua, asonometric reconstruction of sanctuary

on and publication of the site. This is a pity, for it is obviously of great importance, not only because of its own impressive monumentality, but also because of the fascinating parallels its architecture offers to that of the most sophisticated Italian sites. At Munigua, Spanish provincial architecture joins the mainstream. The Emperor-architect Hadrian himself would not need to feel ashamed of it.

Trajan and Hadrian enriched their native peninsula with numerous and impressive public works. Not the least striking of these is the 15-mile aqueduct which served the provincial capital of Tarraco (Fig. 7.6). Its longest surviving stretch (705 feet) bridges a valley just east of the road to Valls, about two and a half miles north of the city. Only Segovia and the Pont du Gard (near Nîmes in the south of France) compare with it in engineering grandeur. It rises on two levels of arches to a height of 92 feet above the valley floor. The lower arches, supported on trapezoidal pylons, give an air of unusual sturdiness. The aqueduct is known locally (in Catalan) as the "Pont del Diable": only the devil himself could have been capable of so daring a construction. The aqueduct is especially handsome at sunset, when its granite blocks seem to turn to gold.

Twelve miles from Tarragona, on the Barcelona road (the ancient Via Herculea Augusta, which the itinerary on the Vicarello cups follows), rises another monument of Trajan's reign, the Arch of Bará (Fig. 7.7). It is 40 feet high, 5 feet lower than the Arch of Titus

FIGURE 7.6
Tarragona, aqueduct

FIGURE 7.7
Bará (Tarragona), Arch of Licinius Sura

in Rome. An inscription upon it gives us some interesting facts about its dedicator, Lucius Licinius Sura, a typical upper civil servant of the time. He was born in the province Tarraconensis, and this is why he made provision in his will (about A.D. 110) to have the arch built here. He had commanded a legion in Germany, been governor of Belgium and later of Lower Germany, been consul three times, and had served his Emperor in his Dacian (Rumanian) Wars (the subject of the reliefs on Trajan's Column in Rome). He was influential in political and literary circles; he had something to do with Hadrian's adoption by Trajan, and he ghost-wrote some of Trajan's speeches; he seems to have been to Trajan what Agrippa had been to Augustus. Pliny the letter writer wrote to him twice, in terms which show Sura to have had a learned and inquiring mind; one of the letters submits for explanation by Sura a couple of hair-raising ghost stories. Sura lived in a mansion on the Aventine Hill in Rome. As befitted an intimate of the Emperor, when he died he was accorded a state funeral, and public baths preserved his memory. He is the type of a provincial who made good.

Farther up the Via Augusta, spanning the River Llobregat 17 miles northwest of Barcelona, is the donkey-backed bridge of Martorell (Fig.

FIGURE 7.8
Martorell, bridge

FIGURE 7.9
Alcántara, bridge

7.8), ancient Tolobi. The train on the Barcelona (Piazza España)-
Iguelda line stops directly beside the bridge. Like the Tarragona aqueduct, it is locally attributed to his Satanic majesty, being called (in
Spanish) the Puente del Diablo. No archaeologist known to me has
dated it, and dating is made more difficult by repeated restorations.
One can only say that its rusticated, pillow-like blocks were in fashion
in Rome in the reign of Claudius (A.D. 41–54) and that it may have
been restored as a part of Trajan's activity in the upkeep of roads and
bridges. Local legend attributes the monumental arch on the left
bank to Hamilcar Barca, Hannibal's father, who distinguished himself
in Spain between 237 and 228 B.C. between the Punic Wars! A modern inscription recording the most recent restoration, under the aus-
pices of Generalissimo Franco, attributes the bridge to Hannibal
himself.

The most famous Trajanic bridge in the world is Alcántara (Arabic:
The Bridge; Fig. 7.9). It lies 36 miles northwest of Cáceres, in spectacular country much haunted by birds: I have spotted there hawks,
owls, storks, swallows, larks, magpies, the gray-backed hooded crow,
hoopoes, flycatchers, bee-eaters, and rollers. The bridge, the highest
in the Roman world (156 feet above the stream), spans a deep granite
gorge cut by the Tagus, on six granite arches, supporting a roadbed

FIGURE 7.10
La Coruña,
lighthouse

630 feet long. The arch in the center once bore an inscription, clamped on by two pairs of bronze hands, dating the bridge in Trajan's fifth consulship (A.D. 103) and naming the 11 municipalities of Lusitania that contributed to its construction. A small shrine at the bridgehead on the Spanish side contains an altar dedicated by one C. Julius Lacer, revered by the Portuguese as their first architect known by name.

At La Coruña (ancient Brigantium), in the far northwest corner of the peninsula, rises a unique monument of Trajan's reign, the only surviving ancient lighthouse in the Roman world (Fig. 7.10). Called for no scholarly reason the Torre de Hercules, it was heavily restored in the eighteenth century, but at least the restoration preserved the lines of the original external stair. It measures 36 Roman feet on a side; its height is 124 Roman feet (in our measure, 33 and 113). An inscription names its architect as another Portuguese, C. Sevius Lupus, from Aeminium (modern Coimbra).

To illustrate Trajanic and Hadrianic public works in the area that is now Portugal, we choose three bridges. The first (Fig. 7.11) is at Chaves in the province of Trás-os-Montes, the ancient Aquae Flaviae, whose name tells us that it was frequented for its hot springs and that it was founded between A.D. 69 and 96. The granite bridge is 450 feet long, supported on 12 massive arches each 19½ feet high. Two milestones at the center of the bridge date it in the same year as Alcántara (A.D. 103).

The second of our Portuguese bridges is that of Vila Formosa (Fig. 7.12), eight and a half miles southwest of Alter do Chão, in Alentejo, on the Roman military road from Emerita to Olisipo (Lisbon). It is 379 feet long and 27 feet high, on six granite arches, with relieving arches and breakwaters. We know that Hadrian destroyed the town in

FIGURE 7.11
Chaves (Trás-os-Montes, Portugal), bridge

FIGURE 7.12
Vila Formosa (Alentejo, Portugal), bridge

FIGURE 7.13
Marvão (Alentejo), bridge

FIGURE 7.14
*Guimarães, Museo Martins Sarmento,
milestone of Tiberius*

A.D. 120, but not whether he destroyed the bridge; it appears in the so-called Antonine Itinerary of Caracalla's reign (A.D. 211–217).

The third bridge is at Portagem, three and a half miles northwest of Marvão, also in Alentejo; the Romans called the place Herminio Minor. It is of no great intrinsic importance and is illustrated (Fig. 7.13) chiefly as a rarity, since it is very seldom reproduced. I can find no scholar who is prepared to date it, but the massive construction and the breakwaters look like workmanship of roughly the same date as the Vila Formosa bridge.

Dozens of milestones in the second volume of the *Corpus of Latin Inscriptions* illustrate the road-building and road-repairing activity of Trajan and Hadrian. The ones I have chosen for illustration come from earlier and later than those reigns. The first (Fig. 7.14) comes from the tiny village of Santa Maria de Panoias, near Braga (the ancient Bracara Augusta), and is now in the museum of the Sociedade

Martins Sarmento in Guimarães. It is dated late in the reign of Tiberius, in A.D. 32 or 33. The other is one of a large series in the Museo Dom Diego de Sousa in the east wing of the old Archbishop's Palace, now the public library, in Braga. The second milestone from the left (Fig. 7.15) is dated in the fourth consulship of the Emperor Caracalla, which fell in A.D. 213.

All the monuments treated in this section—aqueduct, monumental arch, bridges, lighthouse, and milestones—testify to the efficiency with which Roman Emperors and their entourage attended to public works and beautification in their conquered province. The question of generosity does not arise: Trajan made the Lusitanians pay for their own bridge at Alcántara, and other public works for which Emperors took the credit were paid for from the profits of the Spanish mines. But amenities and ease of communications there certainly were—though no Spanish source survives to tell us how far the descendants of the Iberians felt this compensated them for their loss of liberty.

As Mérida is the show town of the Augustan age in Spain, so Italica is the show town of the Hadrianic. It lies some six miles northwest of Seville, in a countryside dotted with white houses, olive and eucalyptus trees, in an air of dusty gold, like a Van Gogh landscape. The great Scipio founded it in 206 B.C. as a place of recuperation for wounded veterans and as Rome's first colony in Spain, an outpost of the Republican Empire. The remains of the Republican colony, and perhaps of the Iberian settlement that preceded it, lie under the adjoining town of Santiponce. Viriathus threatened it in 143 B.C., Sertorius in 79–77 B.C. In 49 B.C. it was for Caesar against Pompey, undeterred by Pompeian atrocities against Caesarians. At Ategua, 84 miles to the east, the bloody-minded Pompeian general Munatius Flaccus killed his enemies' wives before their eyes, had their babies thrown in the air and impaled on spear points, and murdered the men and threw them from the wall.

Italica was rewarded for its loyalty by being granted municipal status, probably under Augustus; this meant that its magistrates were recognized as Roman citizens. Here the future Emperor Trajan was born in A.D. 53; here Hadrian was born in A.D. 76—both from original Italian stock which had emigrated to Spain and achieved status in the local aristocracy. In its present state, Italica is virtually as Hadrian rebuilt it, about A.D. 125. The town surprised Hadrian by requesting

FIGURE 7.15
*Braga,
Biblioteca
Pública,
milestone of
Caracalla*

colonial status, which was usually considered inferior to municipal. The men of Italica wanted it because it involved exemption from land and head tax and because as a colony they could aspire to join, as Hadrian put it, the *effigies parvae simulacraque Romae,* "miniature copies and likenesses of Rome."

Excavation at Italica began early, under the great Spanish pioneer archaeologist Rodrigo Caro in the seventeenth century; Caro also wrote an ode on the ruins. Italica was damaged by the same earthquake that destroyed Lisbon in 1755. In the nineteenth century, the Duke of Wellington himself excavated it, but his excavation notes do not survive. The Romantic movement rédiscovered it; poets recited more odes among its ruins, and this inspired excavation, the results of which have never been published. No attempt was made to prevent stone robbing for road building, and the Countess of Lebrija was allowed to conduct private excavations without government control, with the result that many of the sculptures and mosaics from Italica are immured in the Labrija collection in Seville and closed to public view except by special permission. Worst of all, the government excavations were conducted with a view to finding art treasures—which now enrich the

FIGURE 7.16
Italica, air view

Provincial Museum in Seville—and not to determining strata or dating. This unscientific digging was by no means confined to Spain,* but it remains true that the lack of method made Italica, as a contemporary Spanish archaeologist has called it, "the ruin of a ruin."

But the excavations have revealed ancient Italica as worthy of her grandiose new Hadrianic title: *Colonia Aelia Augusta Italica* (Aelia was Hadrian's family name). The towered walls enclosed a perimeter of just under two miles, in which lived 10,000 people, some of them in houses rich with mosaics, frescoes, and marble. The amphitheater was built to hold 30,000. Everything so far excavated in Italica is on a large and generous scale. With main streets over 52 feet wide, and secondary ones over 45, its city plan was more impressive than

---

* See *The Mute Stones Speak*, p. 26, on vandalism at Etruscan sites in Italy.

that of Pompeii or Ostia, or indeed than that of any contemporary provincial city except Alexandria. The decumanus, which led to the amphitheater outside the walls (see air view, Fig. 7.16), was equipped with sidewalks and drains (high and wide enough for two men to walk abreast) and bordered by shady porticoes. The whole city was laid out on an uncrowded grid plan, with only two houses to a block. One house covered an area of 1,200 square yards (mine, an average professor's house, covers 200). Another has four patios, with mosaics in the master bedroom and even in the latrine (the fight of the pygmies and the cranes). Another has 40 rooms, an exceedingly baroque *impluvium* or rain water tank in the center of the atrium, a fish mosaic in the pool, fountains flanking the dining room, and an entrance screened against heat and cold. Thick walls indicate that the houses—they are really more like palaces—had two stories. One of them had an exedra roofed with a half-dome in concrete, lightened by the insertion of amphoras. But the amphoras were put in the wrong place, and the half-dome collapsed. The rooms were veneered with colored stone: blue-gray, yellow, violet, and white marble, and polished black granite. A tunnel connects the baths with a vaulted cistern.

As befitted so rich a city, Italica had two sets of public baths, at opposite ends of town. One, called for no historical reason the Baños de la Reina Mora (the Baths of the Moorish Queen), has a porticoed patio, separate accommodations for men and women, radiant heating, alabaster dadoes, and a 68-foot pool with an apsidal end. The other, called Los Palacios, is smaller but even more luxurious. Here were found the colossal statues of Trajan and Hadrian now in the Seville museum.

The theater, like the amphitheater, lies outside the walls; it has never been systematically excavated. From it came several pieces of derivative sculpture now in the Seville museum: a Hermes in the fourth-century-Greek style, a Diana, and a voluptuous Venus.

The most spectacular building in Italica is the amphitheater, the fourth largest in the Roman world, next after Rome's, Puteoli's, and Capua's. Overall it measures 508 by 435 feet; its arena is 231 by 150 feet, which makes it about five-sixths the size of the Coliseum in Rome, with nearly twice the seating capacity of Mérida's, and a third again that of Nîmes'. The fabric is concrete, revetted sometimes with brick, sometimes with stone. The five entrances at either end of the long

FIGURE 7.17
Italica,
amphitheater,
cryptoporticus

axis communicate with vaulted tunnels (*cryptoporticus*) which follow
the oval of the plan (Fig. 7.17). These debouch onto stairs to the
seats and to the boxes on the short axes, which were reserved, respec-
tively, for the president and the donor of the games. There is a seven-
foot drop from the balustrade in front of the first row of seats to the
arena level; in the wall thus formed are ten service entrances to the
arena. The seats are divided longitudinally into three sections, the
lowest for the town bigwigs, the knights. In the center of the arena
is a square depression, as at Mérida, brick-lined and containing eight
square pilasters which once supported a wooden roof; a tunnel connects the area with the arena underpinnings (Fig. 7.18). As at Mérida,
this arrangement provided for getting the beasts from their cages into
the arena. Boar's tusks and animal horns were found in the tunnel. The
entrances are vaulted, the walls stuccoed red, the pavement marble or
mosaic, the stairs marble-veneered. The seats have lion's-paw-feet
moulded in stucco. Feet painted red in the pavement have been ex-

FIGURE 7.18
Italica, amphitheater, arena

plained as indicating one-way traffic, or as having some religious significance; they may have combined both functions. The ugly buttresses which support the west side are late additions.

Connected with what went on in the amphitheater is a bronze inscription found in 1888 in what must be the forum area, though it has never been excavated. It is a copy of the minutes of the Senate in Rome in the reign of Marcus Aurelius; the date is A.D. 176–177. It provides maximum prices for first-, second-, and third-class gladiators, ranging downwards from $750 to $150 uninflated, but provides for supplying "condemned criminals" for as little as $100. These "condemned criminals" were almost certainly Christians, whose crime was refusal to worship the philosopher-Emperor.

Italica's aqueduct, which brought water from Sanlúcar la Mayor (Huelva), 24 miles to the west, has been known since 1783. It is noteworthy for being carried not on arches, but on a solid wall.

Italica was a river port, and remains of its mole—masonry, stonework, bronze mooring rings—reported in 1740, have now disappeared. Excavation at its known site would probably uncover warehouses. Its busy traffic is attested by the number of sherds with Italica stamps in Rome's Monte Testaccio. Exports included grain, olive oil, wine, wax, honey, pitch, cochineal, and salt fish—the latter a specialty of the region which has left its archaeological record, to be discussed in the next chapter. The River Baetis (Guadalquivir; the Arabic means the same as the Spanish Rio Grande) changed its course in late antiquity and ruined Italica's trade and prosperity, which then shifted to Hispalis (Seville).

Three extramural necropoleis are known. The one nearest the theater was late, containing both pagan and Christian burials. One skeleton found with the hands cut off may be that of a martyr. There is one of a wife only 13 years old; she was buried with 12 hairpins. Unique are some clay pipes for smoking lavender or drugs—tobacco being, of course, still 1,000 years away.

The finds from Italica include mosaics, sculpture, coins, and inscriptions. The mosaics are partly *in situ*, partly in the Lebrija collection and the Provincial Museum in Seville. They are mostly from pattern-books, but are noteworthy for their number and sumptuousness. There is a fine seasons-mosaic in the Provincial Museum, in which spring is blue-gray; summer, red (it is hot in Andalucia); autumn, gray; and winter, black. An elaborate mosaic in the Lebrija palace includes among its medallions Pan, the rapes of Europa and Ganymede, and Leda and the swan. A fine circus mosaic, now lost and known only from a drawing, has a scene with an overturned chariot, and a limping bareback rider being helped away by a friend. The geometric motifs have been described—by a Frenchman—as "pure Louis XIV": intersecting circles, lozenges, Maltese crosses, thunderbolts, stars, palmettes, crescent-shaped shields, vases, lyres, rosettes, acanthus leaves, knots, hearts.

The sculpture includes a bronze Mercury said to have been made in the fourth century B.C. in Corinth, famous for its bronze work, and to have been sent to Italica by Mummius, who had served against the Lusitanians in Spain before he sacked Corinth in 146 B.C. Another bronze, a Victory, in the Archaeological Museum in Madrid, is a copy of Paeonius' famous fifth-century work in Olympia. An inscription in letters of the second century A.D. memorializes Mummius' gifts. There is a fine head of a young woman, from the amphitheater, now in the Archaeological Museum in Seville. She looks like Augustus' sister Octavia, the most lovable woman of her generation. There is a terracotta head of a woman with an elaborate beehive coiffure which has been identified on slim evidence as Sabina, Trajan's grandniece, who married Hadrian. A bearded likeness of Marcus Aurelius as a priest, veiled for sacrifice—a fold of his toga framing his face—was apparently metaphorphosed in late antiquity into a Christ. A cross is hacked into the breast. There is a particularly effeminate-looking Alexander in the Seville museum, but the effect may be the result of over-enthusiastic cleaning. A particularly supercilious head of a patrician typifies the local aristocracy from which Trajan and Hadrian sprang. On the whole, the collection is chiefly noteworthy for showing what the desire to ape Roman conventions did to the spark of originality in Iberian sculpture.

The coins begin with Augustus (23 B.C.) and end with Theodosius I (A.D. 379–383). The Augustan coins reveal local pride in Roman connections: their symbols are a Roman soldier, the Genius of the Roman People, the wolf, the eagle. In 1898 a hoard of 186 gold coins was found in a goldsmith's house, the latest dated—in modern terms—A.D. 183. It will have been hidden in fear of a raid by the dreaded Italian *condottiere* Maternus, who in A.D. 187 raised a band of adventurers in Italy and marched across Gaul and Spain, sacking and pillaging with impunity. It was a foretaste of things to come.

FIGURE 7.19
*Italica, tile with
first lines of
Virgil's* Aeneid

A collection of 150 inscriptions from Italica awaits publication. One of the most interesting, in the Archaeological Museum in Madrid, is a tile (Fig. 7.19) on which a schoolboy has scratched:

> *Arma virumque cano, Troiae qui primus ab oris
> Italiam, fato profugus, Lavinaque* . . .

These are the first two lines of Virgil's *Aeneid*, and they symbolize the extent to which the Romans placed the stamp of their culture upon this Spanish town.

It is time that we looked into the archaeological evidence for the mines, especially of gold, silver, and copper, from which the Romans derived so much profit in Spain and Portugal. They acquired ownership of the mines by conquest, confiscation, or forced purchase. The state retained control of the precious metals, but allowed the rest to be exploited by individuals and corporations.

The chief source of gold in Roman times was northwest Spain and northern Portugal. The most spectacular site is Las Médulas de Carucedo, on the border between the provinces of Orense and León. Here in their lust for gold the Romans dug pits that would hold a cathedral, and left pyramids of slag 160 feet high, changing the face of the earth so that it looks more like a lunar landscape than a terrestrial one. A dam they constructed to keep the gold-bearing silt from seeping away into the Rio Sil has made an artificial lake 30 miles long. They built the Montefurado tunnel to divert the course of the river and get at the gold-bearing gravel; one nugget weighed 115 grams. They processed 500 million tons of rock for a gold yield of eight grams per ton. Asturica (Astorga) was the gold rush town, an El Dorado and a Johannesburg rolled into one. Slaves—branded, fettered, and working day and night—did the work; when the supply of slaves ran low, the Spanish townsfolk were required to labor in the mines a certain number of days a year; the Emperor Julian (A.D. 361–363) condemned Christians to the mines.

The south of Spain was rich in silver and copper. At El Centenillo, near Castulo (Linares), the vertical shafts went down 650 feet, the horizontal galleries ran 3,000. The shafts were two and a half to three feet in diameter, lined with wood (stamped with the contractor's name) to prevent cave-ins, and supplied with notched oak logs for ladders. The galleries were only three or four feet high; the miners had to work on their hands and knees, putting the ore in esparto-grass baskets which they wore round their necks to keep their hands free for mining.

Some of the equipment used in the mines, on display in the Archaeological Museum in Madrid, is illustrated in Figure 7.20. It comes from Sotiel Coronada (Huelva), in the Rio Tinto copper-mining district, which had been exploited since the palmy days of Tartessus. There are a crucible; wedges; the heads of pick hammers of various sizes; tarred esparto-grass baskets held open with wooden braces for hauling the ore up the vertical shafts or for bailing; sieves; and a set of fetters which tell us that the miners were slaves. Seventeen Celtiberian skeletons were found in the Potosí mine near Guadalcanal (Huelva). Other equipment, not illustrated, included esparto-grass hats, sandals and shin guards, and wooden tallies bearing the miner's name. These were affixed to the ore baskets, to keep track of each miner's output on a piecework basis. In the silver mines, the extracted ore was sifted five times in running water, smelted, and the lead run off.*

---

* For the process, see *The Greek Stones Speak*, pp. 188–189.

FIGURE 7.20
Madrid, Museo Arqueológico Nacional, mining equipment from Sotiel Coronada

Seepage was always a problem in the mines. The Romans solved it by one of two ingenious methods. The first was the Archimedean screw. A set of these was found in El Centenillo. In a wooden container 20 inches in diameter and 14 feet long was set a wooden core eight inches thick, to which copper lugs and rivets attached a helical copper screw an eighth of an inch thick. Its outer edges were attached to the inside of the longitudinal laths of the wooden container. The wooden core ended in iron points pivoting in a timber socket. The container was set on an incline of 30° to 40° and worked by a slave applying his feet to cleats in the middle of the barrel-like container. Each screw would raise the water six feet vertically, depositing it in a square receptacle in which the bottom end of the next screw was set. Waste at intake and discharge amounted to a one-foot loss, so that it would take 20 screws to raise the water 100 feet. If there was a vertical shaft full of water below the bottom screw, an endless belt of esparto grass with buckets attached at intervals would empty the water into the bottom receptacle.

The other method of water disposal was water wheels set in tandem with copper scoops set in the rims. This method worked better in rough-hewn tunnels.

Another interesting gadget is a double-action pump (Fig. 7.21), also from Sotiel Coronada, and also now in Madrid. It consists of two cylinders in which pistons worked alternately up and down, a horizontal tube connecting the two cylinders, and an upright tube inserted into the center of the horizontal one. At the bottom of the cylinders, and on either side of the bottom of the upright tube, were self-acting valves. The lower ends of the two cylinders were immersed in water. The two pistons worked simultaneously but inversely, the one up and the other down. As one piston rose, the valve at the bottom of the cylinder opened and drew in water, while the other piston, descending, closed its own valve and forced the water contained in the cylinder into the horizontal tube, opening the neck valve on its own side and closing the other. The water was thus driven into the upright tube and forced out of it in a continuous stream through the nozzle at the top

FIGURE 7.21

Madrid, Museo Arqueológico Nacional, double-action pump from Sotiel Coronada

which is swiveled to point in any direction. Authorities disagree as to the uses to which this pump was put. One thinks it was used to direct a spray of cold water onto walls against which a fire had been built, thus cracking the face of the seam and facilitating the extraction of the ore. Another supposes that it served as a shower, to cool the sweating backs of the miners. But in the place where it was found, it could only have been used to pump out surplus water.

The copious use of wood in the mines, in shaft liners, pit props, water wheels, screw barrels, ladders, and to feed fires against ore-bearing wall faces, deforested Andalucia and reduced the rainfall, making the mining areas desolate.

One of the most famous Roman mines is in Portugal, at Aljustrel (Alentejo), the ancient Vipasca. The Belgian firm which now mines iron pyrites there is sympathetic to archaeology, and its Portuguese engineer, Octávio da Veiga Ferreira, has made himself an expert on Roman mines. He has excavated a mining-village necropolis of over 500 cremation and inhumation burials (found while excavating for housing for modern workers) which yielded some very handsome glassware, including a bowl with DULCIS VIVAS ("Live *la dolce vita*") in gold between two glass surfaces. He has also dated some of the *terra sigillata* he found there; it is stamped CRESTI, came from south Gaul, and was fired sometime between the reigns of Tiberius and Vespasian (A.D. 14–79). A small museum at the mine houses the finds, including a reconstructed reel like an old-fashioned laundry wringer, for hauling up the ore in baskets; scoops for bailing; notched-log stairs; a bell for marking the beginning and end of shifts; and ingots of copper and of lead.

But the most famous finds from Aljustrel are the two bronze tablets of the *Lex metalli Vipascensis* found in a slag heap at the mine in 1876 and 1906. Both are now in Lisbon, one in the Museo dos Serviços Geológicos, the other in the Museo Etnológico Leite de Vasconcelos, in the suburb of Belém. They date from the reign of Hadrian. They show that the mines and the mining villages were under the control of a resident procurator who administered them as a bailiff would manage an estate. Hadrian encouraged small entrepreneurs by offering special concessions to those who put unopened or abandoned mines into operation. The state owned the mine; the entrepreneur, either individually or acting with others in a corporation, leased it and paid annually half the value of the ore extracted. The lease was forfeit, and put up for auction, if the mine lay idle for six months. The procurator also leased the sources of revenue in the mining village, all of which were state monopolies: auctioneering, running the baths (separate hours for men and women; women to pay double fees), shoemaking, barbering, running fullers' shops, exploiting slag heaps. Schoolmasters, happily, were exempt from taxes. It all shows the infinite Roman capacity for taking bureaucratic pains, and for combining encouragement to initiative with taxing the initiators all they can bear.

Most of the precious metals extracted from the Spanish and Portuguese mines went to Rome, for coinage and for the profit of the Imperial fisc. But some of it stayed in the peninsula, and was made into jewelry: Iberian women still love to deck themselves with gold. The local gold- and silversmiths knew how to solder and to do enameling, granulation, and the filigree work for which the Portuguese are still famous. Their tools have been found: hammers, tweezers, scissors, chisels, burins, punches, polishers, files, saws, bellows, crucibles, molds for making gold wire, scales, compasses, and lathes. So the mines served the small craftsman as well as the Emperor, and one of the end products of the sweat of slaves was the beautification of women.

"If a man were called," wrote Edward Gibbon in a famous passage, "to fix the period in the history of the world during which the condition of the human race was most happy and prosperous, he would, without hesitation, name that which elapsed from the death of Domitian [A.D. 96] to the accession of Commodus [A.D. 180]." The archaeological evidence we have presented in this chapter from Spain and Portugal bears out this rosy view, at least as far as the middle and upper classes were concerned. The axial symmetry of the Munigua sanctuary, the convenience and splendor of the public works and monuments, the luxury of the houses at Italica, the riches pouring out of the ingeniously-equipped and well-administered mines, all add up to a picture of a golden age. The overtaxed and the underprivileged, as usual in archaeology, have left little readable record, apart from the Senate minutes on cheap gladiators, or the pathetic slave fetters from the mines. But, on balance, the evidence is that the Iberians felt themselves well-treated, and indeed archaeological evidence from the next two centuries, to be set forth in the final chapter, tends to show that Spain and Portugal went on, on their own momentum, until the barbarian invasion vandalized the civilization it had taken so many centuries to build.

8
DECLINE
AND
FALL
(A.D. 138–350)

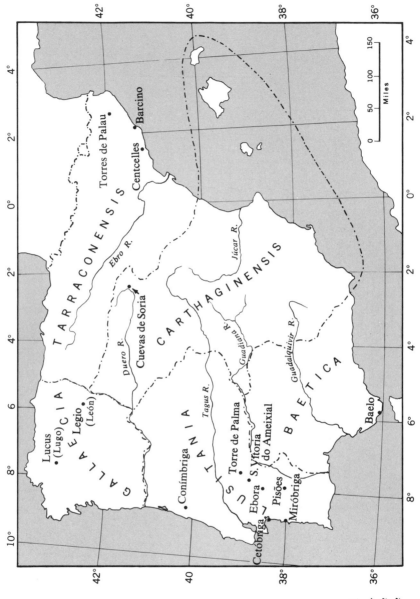

FIGURE 8.1
Iberian Pen-
insula in the
Late Empire

THE DEATH OF HADRIAN IN A.D. 138 DID NOT spell the end of prosperity for his native province. The archaeological evidence is abundant: country villas rich with mosaics (one of them converted in the fourth century to Christian uses), temples, towns, salt-fish factories. But by the middle of the third century the building of massive walls round towns like León, Lugo, and Barcelona reveals the threat of barbarian invasion, and 100 years later Spain is in full decline. The archaeological story of these 200 years is the subject of this chapter.

The soil of the peninsula is particularly rich in villas. For example, in the summer of 1967 I was shown one being excavated and restored at Pisões, six miles southwest of Beja—the ancient Pax Julia—in the Portuguese province of Alentejo (see map, Fig. 8.1). The way to it ran through acre upon acre of wheat. This was the main source also of the wealth which built the villas in antiquity, though wool and the mines, too, had a hand in it. (The countryside in 1967 abounded with gypsies, whom I like to think of as descendants of the migratory workers who reaped the wheat in Roman times.)

The villa has 48 rooms, many of them paved with geometric mosaics; baths with radiant heating; a huge pool; a vivarium (where fish swam until the owner was ready to eat them); stairs with shallow treads; an atrium; and a portico. In a workshop nearby, workmen from

185

Coimbra were doing the careful, ingenious, jigsaw-puzzle work of restoring mosaics. The foreman told me that he had been sent to Pompeii to learn the technique. "But," said he proudly, "I didn't need to go; I knew already." Coins found in the excavation show that the villa was inhabited from the first to the fourth centuries A.D. Since the villa is still unpublished, photographs of it are not permitted.

From the numerous Spanish villas I choose the one at Cuevas de Soria, in pine-clad country, 13½ miles southwest of Soria, in the Numantia area. There is a model of its ground plan, sadly warped, in the Museo de la Diputación in Soria. The one illustrated (Fig. 8.2) is in the Archaeological Museum in Barcelona. The west side, which is plainer, contains the rooms where the workaday life of the farm was carried on; the rest was luxury quarters for the owner. Some of the mosaics are still *in situ*; others are kept in the convent of San Juan de Duero, in Soria. Twenty-two of the villa's 30 rooms had mosaic floors, as did the U-shaped Tuscan-columned corridor around which the rooms were arranged. The mosaic in the *oecus*, the apsidal room in the center of the north wing, is especially fine. Since many of the rooms are divided by cross walls into two-room suites, of which the inner would be especially well protected from cold, one Spanish scholar thinks the villa served in one phase as a *valetudinarium*, or nursing home. With the baths and latrine on a higher level in the southeast corner, the villa overall measures an impressive 260 by 195 feet. Finds of coins show that it was in use from 161 to 340 A.D.

In 1947 a laborer working at Torre de Palma, three miles northwest of Monforte (Alentejo), and 15 miles east of the Vila Formosa bridge, found a column capital which proved to belong to an extremely elaborate *villa rustica*, now the most completely excavated in Portugal. The mosaics, found undermined by ants, were taken up and restored by Italian methods; the best of them are now on display in the Museo Etnológico Dr. Leite de Vasconcelos, next to the monastery of the Jerónimos, in the suburb of Lisbon called Belém. The buildings cover an area of 325 by 300 feet, with baths and a farm wing on the west and the master's block on the northeast. The villa was planned to be cool in summer, warm in winter. It commanded an extensive view across the endless plain to the west, to foothills sheltering other villas to the south and southeast. Cicadas fill the air with their sawing at noonday, frogs with their croaking at twilight; in between, one hears the honking of swans and geese.

FIGURE 8.2
Barcelona, Museo Arqueológico Provincial, model of villa at Cuevas de Soria

The farm buildings contained the bailiff's quarters, the oil and wine store, slave quarters, stables, barn, kitchen, and sheepfold. The master's quarters were more luxurious, with rooms for all seasons, an opulent table, a silver service (not found) for a proprietor obviously—from the mosaics—devoted to the arts and to sport, a lover of tradition and the good life, surrounded by relatives, flattering friends, clients, and servants, inviting his equally wealthy neighbors to gourmet dinners of oysters, fish, chilled wine, and game. (Ancient Lusitania was obviously not an area of absentee landlords.) His imported *terra sigillata*, and his bronze lamps were of the type in use in the second century A.D. We can imagine that his summer garden was planted with roses, violets, and lilies; that after a workout in his exercise grounds he could stroll in their covered walks and then bathe in baths planned to face the afternoon sun, and enjoy the services of a masseur and a hair dyer. It was a villa luxuriously planned for enjoying *la dolce vita*.

The most striking thing about the villa is the huge mosaic from the tablinum. It measures 33 by 20 feet, and its 11 pictured panels span the mosaicist's repertory. Of the two largest, one, rectangular, portrays the nine muses, each in a colorful costume differently draped, and many with their attributes: Erato, the muse of love poetry, carries a lyre; Melpomene, muse of tragedy, carries a mask and wears elevator shoes. Beneath is an inscription instructing the slaves to sweep the floor carefully and not harm the mosaic.

The other large rectangular panel portrays a Bacchic cortège. The god, with Ariadne and satyrs, rides in a chariot drawn by meek but colorful tigers, escorted by a goat-footed Pan, a nude satyr with a goat-skin, and maenads brandishing tambourines and carrying the baskets that contained the sacred objects used in initiation.

The two large rectangular mosaics enclose another series of eight square ones, containing conventional figures like a fat, drunken Silenus; a Daphne already half-metamorphosed into a laurel, gesturing before a bored Apollo; Medea with a particularly revolting child; a Marlon Brando mad Hercules, about to slay his minute children while his

FIGURE 8.3
Lisbon (Belém),
Museo Etnográfico
Leite de
Vasconcelos,
Theseus-Minotaur
mosaic, from Torre
de Palma villa
(Alentejo)

wife looks pensively on. In a larger panel, outside the set described, a muscular Theseus (Fig. 8.3), brandishing a club, holds by one horn a particularly craven Minotaur, with the body of a pugilist and the head of a bull, who grasps his conqueror round the leg with one arm, suppliant-fashion; the other arm he raises over his head to cry quits.

An adjoining room contains mosaic likenesses of five named prize race horses. The one in the center is prancing spiritedly, as though he were treading grapes; he wears a collar of bells. All these mosaics are amusing but provincial. One can see that the proprietor of Torre de Palma had money; it is not so clear that he had taste.

At Santa Vitória do Ameixial, 18 miles southwest of Torre de Palma, a little girl who had been to the museum in Lisbon and seen some mosaics recognized some on her father's farm and notified the authorities. The result was the discovery of another luxury villa with a complete repertory of mosaics: flowers, meander patterns, fauna, masks, seasons, months, winds, gods, myths, athletes. Excavation was informal, and its publication delayed for 40 years: the excavator reports that he was "shown, but not given" a gold coin of the reign of Nero; other coins date the life of the villa from the second to the fourth centuries A.D. It lies some five and a half miles north of the main Roman road from Emerita to Olisipo; if the whole stretch from the villa to the road belonged to its owner, it was a very sizable estate. Its crops were grain (as proved by finds of granite millstones) and wine (as proved by finds of amphoras). Spades, picks, sickles, and trowels were among the objects excavated. Stones from the villa in re-use are to be seen all over the village, in seats, tables, floors, the local fountain, and the cemetery wall. Among the mosaics, now in the Lisbon (Belém) museum, one of Ulysses and the sirens recalls the sculpture from the Villa of Tiberius at Sperlonga in Italy.* There is another Bacchus mosaic, this time not with tigers, but with panthers flanked by dolphins. There are some athletes like those from the Baths of Caracalla in Rome. In the most extraordinary one of all a man attacks a naked woman who is covering her private parts; an inscription mysteriously appeals to Proserpina, goddess of the underworld. Could the villa owner have been masochistic enough to commission a portrait of his wife taken in adultery?

----

* See *The Mute Stones Speak*, pp. 175–176.

FIGURE 8.4

Barcelona, Museo Arqueológico Provincial, circus mosaic from Torres de Palau

Moving back from Portugal to Spain, we find in the Museo Arqueológico Provincial in Barcelona a mosaic from Torres de Palau (Gerona) with another favorite scene: chariot racing in the Circus Maximus in Rome. The Roman scene is set by the representations of Romulus and Remus suckled by the wolf and Mars about to seduce Rhea Silvia (Fig. 8.4, right). Next, to the left, the *carceres* (starting gates) lie open. The race has begun; it is a tight race, with a serious accident, chariot and horses both topsy-turvy. Charioteers and horses are named; the aficionados went wild over their favorites, even as far away as Rome. Down the middle of the course runs the *spina*, adorned with statues, trophies, markers for the laps, and an obelisk which dates the mosaic before A.D. 357.* Below the mosaic in the Barcelona museum is a model, made from it, of the Circus Maximus in Rome (Fig. 8.5).

The wealth so evident in rich private villas is reflected also in public buildings, like the temple at Évora (ancient Ebora), the best-

---

* See *The Mute Stones Speak*, p. 333 (Circus mosaic, Piazza Armerina, Sicily).

preserved temple in Portugal (Fig. 8.6), commonly, but without authority, called the Temple of Diana. Its granite columns with their marble Corinthian capitals stand on a high granite podium. Its dimensions (80 by 50 feet) are almost the same as those of the Maison Carrée in Nîmes, which Thomas Jefferson used as the model for his State House in Richmond, Virginia. Used as a fort in the Middle Ages, it served in the nineteenth century as an abattoir; it was not cleared of excrescences until 1870. Its date is Severan (A.D. 193–235).

The beauty of excavating Roman remains in Portugal is that it tells us so much about country places that are never mentioned in literature. The cities—Lisbon (Olisipo), Coimbra (Aeminium), Porto (Portus Cale)—have Roman underpinnings, too, but it is impossible to move large populations to get at the remains. So excavation goes on in smaller places, and very revealing it is; for example, at Miróbriga (Santiago do Cacém [Setúbal]) halfway along the Roman—which is also the modern—road from Lisbon to Lagos (Lacóbriga) on the south coast, "the westernmost road in the Roman Empire," at the turnoff for Beja (Pax Julia) and Seville (Hispalis). The comfortable government *pousada* (hotel) at Santiago do Cacém probably occupies the site of the *mansio*, or posthouse, on the ancient Roman road.

FIGURE 8.5

Barcelona, Museo Arqueológico Provincial, model of Circus Maximus in Rome, made from mosaic, figure 8.4

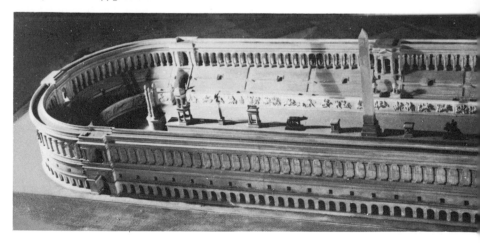

As early as the seventeenth century, the notorious Portuguese antiquarian and forger André de Resende (1498–1573), who liked to invent contacts between Portuguese places and famous Romans like Sertorius and Caesar, was publishing inscriptions allegedly from Miróbriga. In the early nineteenth century, M. de Cenáculo, Bishop of Beja from 1777 to 1802, who tracked down inscriptions relentlessly, and copied them accurately, excavated at the site; a sculptured hand which he found and took to Beja turned out to fit some sculptured fingers found in 1944; they are now all happily reunited in the local museum in Santiago do Cacém. Part of the archaeological bishop's collection of inscriptions was once housed in the temple at Évora. Since 1959 Miróbriga has been the site chosen as a training ground for young Portuguese and foreign archaeologists. The results have been most fruitful: yet another terraced sanctuary, like Mulva; baths; a bridge; a circus (the only one excavated in Portugal); houses frescoed in Pompeian red, blue-gray, and yellow; datable molded pottery (from Augustus through Commodus); fragments of sculpture; coins; 34 inscriptions; and the usual humble objects of everyday use—pins, needles, awls, pitchforks, mattocks, bits, and chisels. The bath complex is quite clear in the right center of the aerial photograph (Fig. 8.7), but the picture was taken before the excavation of the terraced sanctuary on the arx, which therefore appears only as crop marks on the hills in the lower left corner.

In Figure 8.8 we are standing on the middle of three terraces, which is the level of a paved court which originally had a portico on three sides commanding a magnificent view across the Alentejo plain. The stairs to the left lead to an apsidal sanctuary on the upper level, perhaps of Venus (on the evidence of an inscription). Beyond the stair runs the back wall of the court, into which projects the podium of another temple, perhaps of the healing-god Aesculapius (another inscription). Where the podium meets the wall of the court there is a stair. (There is another stair axially symmetrical to it, but not visible in the photograph, on the other side of the podium.) The front corner of the podium is scooped out in a quarter-circle; the podium's front wall has two rectangular niches in it to relieve the flatness. Beyond these, on the far front corner, out of the photograph, comes the scooped quarter-circle again. The temple itself is central on its podium and on the axis of the court. The parallel with Munigua is obvious.

FIGURE 8.6
Evora, temple

Pottery fragments found in the terrace area are dated in the third century A.D.; above them is a burnt level which belongs to the period of the barbarian invasions 100 years later.

Flanking the court are Roman houses; at its front (southeast) corner a steep stair leads down to the third terrace level, also occupied by houses. Two paved roads also swing down the hill and meet (Fig. 8.9) at the baths. Aesculapius being the god of health, the baths may have been therapeutic, fed through lead pipes from medicinal hot springs. Their component parts are visible in the aerial photograph. The round area is a cistern; to the right of it is a dressing room and latrine, set over running water. The L-shaped area is a vestibule and exercise ground opening to the right into a cold plunge, a warm bath

FIGURE 8.7

Miróbriga (Santiago do Cacém, Portugal), air view

FIGURE 8.8
Miróbriga, terraced sanctuary

with apsidal steam room adjoining, and a hot bath, also apsidal, which finishes off the complex on the far right. Walls and floor had radiant heating; * there were frescoes and marble veneer. The running water which flushed the latrine came from a stream spanned by a single-arched Roman bridge. A nearby house yielded coins of Emperors who reigned between A.D. 238 and 251, which dates the area in the mid-third century, about the same time as the terraced sanctuary above. The major part of the town, including the forum and necropolis, has yet to be found and excavated.

About a kilometer southeast of the baths are the remains of the circus, nearly 1,100 feet long and 240 feet wide, with a capacity of 25,000. Since this is nearly four times the population of the present town, and therefore surely much larger than the modest size of ancient Miróbriga would require, the conclusion is obvious that the place was a center of rustic pilgrimage, and the circus planned for capacity seasonal crowds, especially at the five-day festival in honor of Aesculapius in the spring—of which we know from an inscription. The rest of the time the track was used for tryouts. Lusitania was famous

---

* See *The Mute Stones Speak*, pp. 257–258 (Forum Baths, Ostia).

for its charioteers: Diocles, the most famous one in the Roman world, was born in Lusitania, and retired in Rome in A.D. 146 at the age of 42 after an unprecedented total of 1,462 victories in 4,257 starts—an average of 177 races a year in his 14-year career—for a total purse of 3,770,000 sesterces ($188,888 uninflated). He could drive a team of seven horses abreast. Since only two circuses are known in Portugal (the other never excavated), Diocles may well have run some of his youthful tryouts here. The track was in use for nearly 200 years after his retirement; the excavator dates the stonework of its latest phase to the late third or early fourth century. By this time the rivalry among the four stables—the Reds, Whites, Blues, and Greens —had assumed, even in high places, even more importance than a pennant race among American sports fans. Gibbon describes with eloquent scorn how the worst Emperors encouraged their chosen color: "They frequented their stables, applauded their favourites, chastised their antagonists, and deserved the esteem of the populace by the natural or affected imitation of their manners."

One of the fragmentary inscriptions found at Miróbriga mentions the Emperor Aurelian (A.D. 270–275), one of whose claims to fame is the still-surviving wall he built around the city of Rome.* His reign falls in a time of trial, the archaeological evidence for which takes the form of city walls all over the Empire, including Spain, where the best-preserved circuits are in León, Lugo, and Barcelona.

León is what is left in Spanish of the Latin word *legio*. The ill-fated Galba, who was Emperor for six months in A.D. 68–69, founded it as a camp for his Spanish legion, VII Gemina Pia Felix, in a strategic spot in a thickly inhabited area (ancient population 240,000)—its function to protect the mines. Work is now going on to locate the wall of this first phase. The section now visible (Fig. 8.10), partly mediaeval, belongs to a circuit built about A.D. 250 which covered an area of 1,753 by 1,050 feet. The surviving stretch is 18 feet thick, with 31 towers, each 27 feet high.

The walls of Lugo (Fig. 8.11), ancient Lucus Augusti (the grove of Augustus), date from Aurelian's reign. They are the only walls in the Roman world which one can walk or ride completely around on

---

* See *The Mute Stones Speak*, pp. 321–326.

top. They are revetted with local slate, with granite at the gates. Their circuit is a mile and a quarter; they are 20 feet thick, 35 to 45 feet high, and include 78 towers, so close together that we conclude the defense plans did not envisage the use of the long-range ballista.

FIGURE 8.9
Miróbriga, Roman road at baths

FIGURE 8.10
León, wall

The most interesting late-Roman city in Spain—because it has been so carefully excavated—is Barcelona. Archaeologists have traced its history unbroken from Neolithic times. The Roman city produced no Emperors nor literary lights. After the Cantabrian War, Augustus settled veterans there; in the early Empire it was a comfortable bourgeois town, *Colonia Julia Augusta Paterna Faventia Barcino*, ranked eighth in importance in Spain (not as an administrative but as an economic center), noted for the wealth of its inhabitants, the security of its port, and the fertility of its hinterland—a symbol of the *pax Romana* in a modest provincial city. Then, in the early 260s A.D., all hell broke loose. Threatened by an invasion of Franks and Alemanni—who still invade annually as tourists—the citizens, in a frenzy, destroyed more monuments than the barbarians would

FIGURE 8.11
Lugo, wall and gate

have. They needed the stone to build an emergency wall, which enclosed an area much smaller than the previously inhabited zone: only 30 acres, not even including the port (the new wall would protect only about 3,500 people). The district is now the picturesque old quarter of Barcelona, the "barrio gótico"; it contains the Cathedral —built over an early Christian basilica—and the Diputación and Ayuntamiento, headquarters of the provincial and municipal administration (see plan, Fig. 8.12, and air view, Fig. 8.13, in which north is at the right). These buildings face on the Plaza San Jaime, which was the forum of the third-century city.

The wall, nearly 30 feet high, had a perimeter of only 3,900 feet; but it was equipped, at intervals of 20 to 26 feet, with no less than 78 towers, mostly square, but octagonal or round at the gates and

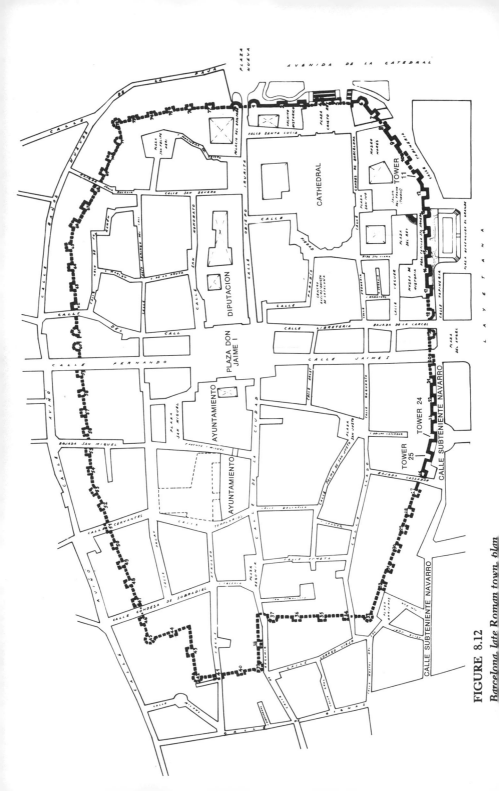

FIGURE 8.12
Barcelona, late Roman town plan

FIGURE 8.13
Roman Barcelona, air view

where the wall changed direction. Some stretches have been lovingly restored, especially on the north in front of the Cathedral (Fig. 8.14): the round tower forms the left side of a gate, and the abutting arch is a part of the Roman aqueduct. The arched windows are ballista-slits.

Since 1957 the municipal authorities of Barcelona have been excavating just inside the wall and within the towers. They have found that the panic-stricken inhabitants of the threatened Roman town threw into the fill of the towers whatever stone they could lay their hands on, including works of art. Figure 8.15 shows the interior of Tower 11 (see plan) where in the winter of 1959 the excavators found the togaed torso of one statue, the feet of another, and the head of a third. Eighteen months later, in excavating the interior of Tower 24, they found, in what looked like soft earth but was really hard mortar, a headless bust which had to be excavated with bronze tools to avoid damaging the marble. Figures 8.16 and 8.17 show the bust in two stages of excavation. It proved to fit onto the head from Tower 11 and to be a likeness of Faustina the Younger, who in A.D. 145 married the philosopher-Emperor Marcus Aurelius.

FIGURE 8.14
Barcelona, late Roman wall

FIGURE 8.15
Barcelona, interior of tower, with head of bust in figures 8.16 and 8.17

Tower 25, in the well-preserved stretch along the Calle Subteniente Navarro (see plan), is built up from a very finely carved molding (Fig. 8.18). But where the tower joins the wall there is another molding with a different profile, betraying the fact that both are the cornices of older buildings, in re-use upside down.

In a model installation (Fig. 8.19), the excavations of Roman houses under the Museo de la Ciudad have been roofed over and opened to the public. Conspicuous are two columns of an atrium and the impluvium, lined with waterproof cement (*opus signinum*). Also under the museum are the remains of a Visigothic wall which contains older stones in re-use. Figure 8.20 shows two blocks of a relief of togaed figures carrying staffs of office; they are probably lictors with the fasces, in attendance upon a magistrate. Figure 8.21 shows another part of the wall, with an inscription built into it. The *cognomina*, Achilleus and Eutychanus, are both Greek, the names of

FIGURE 8.16   FIGURE 8.17
Barcelona, marble bust, first phase   Barcelona, marble bust, second phase
of excavation   of excavation

freedmen; but the *nomen*, Julius, is Latin, the name of one of the
noblest clans of all; the ancestors of these men will have been freed
by Augustus, and have taken his clan name in gratitude. Barcelona
has yielded over 200 inscriptions altogether, bearing the names of 300
citizens; the evidence of the names is that the city was a melting
pot. The richer citizens were public-spirited: one built a set of public
baths and provided a gift of olive oil for the citizens on his birthday;
another is the first known Spaniard to have won in the Olympic
games (A.D. 129)—in keeping with the peninsula's reputation, the
event won was the chariot race.

In the Museo Arqueológico (*not* the Museo de la Ciudad) of Barcelona there is a portico (Fig. 8.22) reconstructed from the remains
of a large building of the second century A.D., with Corinthian capitals,
a fascia, and an architrave with a serpentine design. It used to be

FIGURE 8.18
Barcelona, Tower 25, cornice in re use

FIGURE 8.19
Barcelona, Roman houses under Museo de la Historia de la Ciudad

FIGURE 8.20
(*above*)
*Barcelona,
Roman relief in
Visigothic wall*

FIGURE 8.21
(*left*)
*Barcelona,
Roman
inscription in
Visigothic wall*

FIGURE 8.22

Barcelona, Museo Arqueológico Provincial, reconstructed portico

thought that this portico came from the Roman theater, but the best guess now is that it was probably a funerary monument.

The model in the glass case to the left of the portico is of a temple, three columns of which (Fig. 8.23) survive in the Calle Paradis (street but not temple shown in plan, Fig. 8.12). The capitals are of the Composite order, and the moldings are of the sort in vogue in the Julio-Claudian period (A.D. 14–68). The temple may have been the Capitolium, or dedicated to Rome and Augustus. It dates from a time two centuries before the rather pathetic walls were built, a time when the colony was in its prime, its future not all behind it.

The next two sites to be described both have to do with a specialty of the Iberian peninsula, the making of a fish sauce called *garum*, as much appreciated by ancient gourmets as caviar is today. Both sites are late; the earlier, Cetóbriga (Setúbal/Troia, in Portugal), is dated by an amazing hoard of 18,181 coins, found in 1957, at about A.D. 300. In the town the remains of a *garum* factory were found. Across the bay (the estuary of the River Sado) from Setúbal, the long sandspit of Troia, once an island, covers most of the remains of what was either a suburb of Cetóbriga, or the main town, in Roman times; it was the point of export for the copper mined at Vipasca (Aljustrel). It is accessible by ferry, but at high tide the ruins themselves can only be reached by rowboat across a creek. The trip is well worthwhile for the sake of the waterproof concrete vats for making *garum* which are to be seen there (Fig. 8.24). One hundred years ago there were over 2,000 of these vats, extending along the shore for about three miles.

For salting, and the making of *garum*, the favorite fish was tuna, which still abounds in south Spanish and Portuguese waters. Then, as now, a lookout in a watchtower, noticing the color and movement of a school of tuna in the water, would alert the fishermen, who rowed out to their fixed nets into which the fish blundered and were slaughtered, turning the water red with blood. The catch was taken to salting huts, where fins, heads, innards, and roe were removed. Then the flesh was cut up, salted, and stacked in layers in brine tanks like the larger ones at Troia. This stage of the process took three weeks; the end product was sealed in amphoras. *Garum* was made from the scraps: crushed flesh and roe steeped in the smaller tanks, then left in containers in a warm room to evaporate the brine. When the paste had cooled it was sealed in jars and exported to gourmets all over the Mediterranean.

The other site where a *garum* factory has been found is Baelo (Bolonia [Cádiz]) a few kilometers west of Tarifa, near the entrance to the Straits of Gibraltar. Its excavators (1917–1922) were Pierre Paris (who got the Dama de Elche for the Louvre) and George Bonsor, the excavator of the necropolis at Carmona. They found two *garum* establishments; later excavation has unearthed three more. "Unearthed" is the right word: the factories lay outside the south edge of the city wall (see plan, Fig. 8.25), and the strong east wind had covered them with from two to four meters of sand. One establishment had 15 concrete vats, in two rooms separated by an area for cleaning the fish, with a waterproof floor sloped for ease in swabbing it down.

FIGURE 8.23

Barcelona, Capitolium or Temple of Rome and Augustus

There is more to Baelo than *garum* factories. The owner's house adjoined his factory on the east, sharing one wall with it; he must have been inured to the smell. The house is a late, makeshift affair (dated from coins A.D. 337–350); the bases of some of the peristyle columns were made of second-hand capitals set upside down. But the walls were stuccoed Pompeian red, and one room had frescoes by a local artist whose hand Bonsor also recognized in the Baelo necropolis. East of the atrium was a vestibule flanked by shops; in order to avoid the prevailing wind and insure privacy, the door from atrium to vestibule is not on the same axis as the steps from the vestibule to the colonnaded street.

The house across the street had its porter's lodge paved in purple, and its room walls were a wild riot of non-decorator colors. One had an imitation marble dado, with bands of red and green above; and,

FIGURE 8.24
Troia (Setúbal, Portugal), **garum** *vats, reconstructed*

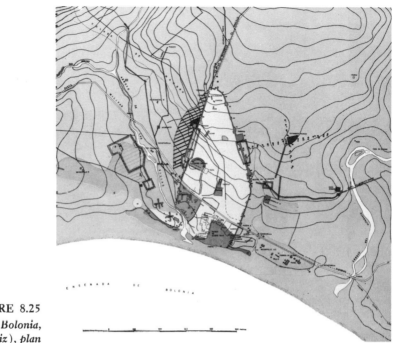

FIGURE 8.25
*Baelo (Bolonia,
Cádiz), plan*

above them, red panels crossed by white lines enclosing unidentifiable bright yellow motifs. Another room had flowers painted in the corners of the panels, and a red-brown frieze with flowers and swags in white and green. The peristyle columns were stuccoed white and veined with yellow to imitate marble. In the kitchen, a secondhand sundial—which in its Roman form was a square block of stone scooped out spherically at the top—was in re-use as a stove. Paris found *graffiti* on the walls: pornographic verse, and a sketch of a gladiator striding along with a trident, gauntlet gloves, shin-guards, and a huge helmet.

The colonnaded street between the *garum*-factory house and the sundial house was 32 feet wide, including the sidewalks, and led through a gate in the wall on an axial line to the forum and Capitolium, the central one of three temples, with lions' head cornices and a long pedestal within for statues of magistrates. Paris found the forum in use as a threshing floor; the theater as a pigsty. Its seating is not fitted into a natural slope, in the Greek fashion, but is built up with masonry, in the Roman. Nowadays from the seats there is a magnificent view across the Straits of Gibraltar to the mountains of Africa, but in antiquity the stage buildings blocked the vista.

Baelo's main aqueduct ran on arches with pierced piers and entered from the west at the level of the forum. It ran in pipes hollowed out of solid stone and discharged into a vaulted cistern. Paris complains that he had no explosives to blast out the enormous fallen blocks of the vault in order to explore the cistern. It is no wonder that he has nothing to say about stratigraphy, and little about dating. He publishes, on the other hand, a remarkable number of photographs of his small daughter in a *very* French hat.

Bonsor, who had had experience at Carmona, excavated the two necropoleis, one to the east of the town wall, the other to the west. The 1,189 burials (only a quarter of the probable total) make Baelo second only to Carmona in importance among Roman cemeteries in Spain. The finds, remarkable especially for the very fine glassware, are in the Archaeological Museum in Madrid. More glassware was found than is on display: Bonsor reports that much of it powdered into dust on exposure to the air. Careless workmen broke many a pot, and small finds escaped notice because no one had thought to provide a sieve. But what Bonsor found was of fascinating variety: coffers, coins, mirrors, tear-vases, awls, needle boxes, ear-picks, depilatory pincers, styluses, spatulas, fishhooks, rings, an ivory comb, a necklace with a silver amulet, jewelry in rock crystal, cornelian, amber, and faïence, the remains of offerings of chickens, eggs, and pine nuts. The cremation ashes and bones were enclosed in pots which were potters' rejects; the pots in turn contained glass jars; adhering to the sides of the jars Bonsor found bits of the linen in which the bones had been wrapped. He also found the remains of the ivory or iron legs of the biers on which the corpses were cremated. Children were buried, not cremated. Bonsor found the skeleton of one child with seven mint-fresh nails around it, perhaps one for each year of the child's short life. The representations of the dead on the *stelae* over the graves Bonsor—who was an artist—found so impossibly bad that he wondered if the provincial sculptors had ever seen a human face. Yet at least the carvings were not conventional provincial Roman; they are the decadent descendants of the great Iberian sculpture of Cerro de los Santos. Bonsor reports (Paris disagreeing) some evidence of men buried alive or after a violent death; he found skeletons which had been thrown into pits; some landed sitting or bent-legged; others have

their bony hands over their mouths, their stomachs, or their private
parts. The necropoleis were in use over a long period; some of the
terra sigillata from the graves bear the marks of potters who were
working in the period from Claudius to Vespasian (A.D. 41–79); on
the other hand, the use of the same painter for the *garum*-factory
house wall and the wall of a tomb dates the tomb in the mid-fourth
century A.D., the same date as the latest coins found in the house.
Barbarians had cultivated no taste for *garum*, and this is a partial
explanation for Baelo's decline and fall.

FIGURE 8.26
Conímbriga (Condeixa-a-Velha, Portugal), plan

FIGURE 8.27
Conímbriga, hunt mosaic

Another piece of archaeological evidence of panic in the face of the barbarian threat comes from Conímbriga (modern Condeixa-a-Velha), nine miles south of Coimbra, in Portugal. Here a massive but hastily-built wall, full of inscribed blocks and truncated statues, was thrown up about A.D. 305; the evidence for the date is a milestone of Constantius Chlorus, father of Constantine the Great, Caesar of the West from A.D. 293 to 306. The line of the wall cut through an elaborate complex of villas (see plan, Fig. 8.26) which were revealed by excavation for a tourist road in 1939. The villas have *impluvia* and *nymphaea* of contorted, baroque outline. The mosaic floors are particularly rich, even those of geometric design, in vivid polychrome with variegated panels and rope-like swags which anticipate the Portuguese "Manueline" style of the great days of Prince Henry the Navigator, Vasco da Gama, and Magellan. There is also an amusing genre scene, in which a groom leads a bald, potbellied, drunken Silenus on a donkey. In another mosaic, the hero Perseus brandishes at a delightful open-mouthed dragon—it looks like a large worm—the head of Medusa, freshly severed with his sword, whose scabbard hangs above. The villas resemble in luxury the previously mentioned imperial hunting lodge near Piazza Armerina in Sicily. Here, as there, the excavators found a hunting mosaic (Fig. 8.27), in which four mounted horsemen pursue a stag, while other quarry—they look like guinea hens—lurk in the corners of the square which encloses the central medallion. Excavation is continuing at Conímbriga: I visited it in late August 1967, at the moment when workmen were digging out a bath (it belongs in the blank lower left corner of the plan, Fig. 8.26) which had been discovered only the week before.

Ancient Conímbriga gave its name, in the Middle Ages, to the modern university city of Coimbra, but there is a possibility of confusion here, because Coimbra's ancient name was Aeminium. A city of 45,000 does not lend itself to overall excavation, but there is an impressive series of cryptoporticoes, on three levels, under the Museo Machado de Castro. It was the podium for a military headquarters, or for the forum. The nearby church of S. João de Almeida has been built into the ruins of a Roman temple. The plans may have been drawn by the Lusitanian architect Sevius Lupus, who came from here.

This book is conceived as a selective chronological survey of secular archaeology in Spain and Portugal; references to Christianity have been deliberately incidental: the baptistery in the apsidal house at Mérida; Christian burials in pagan necropoleis. But we have come now to the fourth century A.D., by which time Christianity has become as much a part of the Iberian scene as the barbarian menace. It is fitting that we should close with a pagan monument metamorphosed into a Christian one. Such a monument the German Archaeological Institute in Madrid has been excavating at Centcelles, on the old Roman road to Caesaraugusta (Zaragoza), three miles northwest of Tarragona. It is a villa, perhaps built for Constantine the Great, with a cupola mosaic; it was transformed in the mid-fourth century into a mausoleum, perhaps for Constans, Constantine's son, who was murdered at Autun, 150 miles away, in A.D. 350. (The nearest village to the site is called Constantí.)

The mosaics are in three concentric circles. In the innermost, the seasons are represented as Cupids, and a woman leads a child to a figure on a throne. In the middle ring are scenes from the Old and New Testament: Adam and Eve, Daniel in the lions' den, Jonah, the Good Shepherd, Noah's ark, the worship of the golden calf, the resurrection of Lazarus, the three men in the fiery furnace. The outermost ring is a hunting scene. We see the preparations for the hunt, the

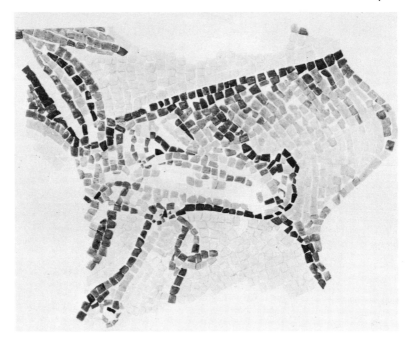

FIGURE 8.28
Centcelles (Constantí, Tarragona), stag from hunt mosaic

beaters with net and stakes, the hounds on leash; next, the stags (Fig.
8.28) being driven into the net, with cloth "scares" hanging from ropes
to frighten them by their fluttering; finally, the happy homecoming of
hunters on horseback and afoot, against a background of city and
palace. It looks like a unique union of pagan and Christian motifs,
but probably the inner and the outer circles are Christian symbols,
too. The hunt would then be a figure of the earthly life; and the
happy homecoming the reception of the Christian soul into heaven.

We began with the hunt, in the splendid animals from the Palaeolithic cave at Altamira, and it is fitting that we should end with it,
in the mosaics from Conímbriga and Centcelles. Four hundred and
six generations of men separate the prehistoric from the late Roman
works of art. If the prehistoric seems better than the late Roman,
archaeology has once again done its frequent service, upsetting fixed

ideas, such as the idea of progress. The simple huts of Briteiros, Coaña, and Numantia, the beetling walls of Tarragona will remind us of the long, brave tradition of Spanish resistance; but just as we are about to resolve that the Romans were villains, the walls of Ampurias, dismantled for the view, are there to remind us of the blessings of the Roman Peace, a reminder reinforced by the amenities of the theater at Mérida, the amphitheater at Italica, and the Alcántara bridge. Just as we are tempted by the crude barrel relief or the conventional Augustus from Mérida to dismiss provincial art as conventional or derivative, we remember the Gran Dama Oferente from Cerro de los Santos, the Dama de Elche, or the strong-faced proprietress of the villa at Ampurias, and are not prepared to generalize so shallowly. Archaeology, as always the handmaid of history, has told us a little more about man's past, which has made his present and will shape his future. Another, and not unimportant, chapter of intellectual history is written, when archaeology makes the Iberian stones speak.

Acknowledgments

Barcelona
    Bosch, Casa Editorial: 6.3
    Instituto Gallach: 1.6, 1.8, 2.4–5, 5.6
    Ediciones Labor: 5.11
    Foto Mas: 3.3, 3.5, 4.10, 4.14, 6.2, 6.4, 6.6, 6.12, 6.13, 7.6
    Museo Arqueológico Provincial: 1.2, 1.5, 1.7, 1.12, 2.10–11, 3.6–9, 4.20,
        8.2, 8.4–5, 8.22
    Museo de la Historia de la Ciudad: 8.12–21, 8.23
    Verrié: 1.3–4

Berlin
    Deutsches archäologisches Institut: 1.9

Gerona
    Diputación Provincial: 4.2–5, 4.9

Guimarães
    Foto Beleza: 4.24, 4.31–32

Lisbon
    Academia de Belas Artes: 7.12–13, 8.6
    Fundaçao Calouste Gulbenkian: 5.8
    D. Fernando de Almeida: 8.7
    M. Heleno: 8.3
    A. do Paço: 1.10

London
    G. Bell & Sons: 6.10

Madison, Wisc.
    University of Wisconsin Cartographic Laboratory: 1.1, 2.1, 3.1, 4.1,
    6.18, 7.1, 8.1

Madrid
    M. Almagro: 3.2
    Arquivo Español de Arqueologia: 2.3
    Consejo Superior de Investigaciones Científicas: 2.2
    Deutsches archäologisches Institut: 3.4, 4.21, 4.36, 6.14, 6.19, 7.2–5,
    7.10–11, 8.9, 8.11, 8.25, 8.28
    Dirección General del Turismo: 3.12, 6.8, 6.16, 7.9, 7.17–18
    Espasa-Calpe: 2.6, 4.23, 4.29, 5.1, 5.3–5, 5.7, 5.9–10, 5.14, 6.7, 6.9,
    6.11, 6.15, 7.17, 8.26
    A. García y Bellido: 4.30, 6.17, 7.16
    Museo Arqueológico Nacional: 2.7–9, 2.12, 4.11–13, 4.15–19, 6.1,
    7.19–21

Mérida
    Museo Arqueológico Provincial: 6.5

New York
    Casa de Portugal: 7.15
    Hispanic Society of America: 6.20

All other photographs are by the author

Books and Articles Consulted

1 / *From the Cave Man to the Bronze Age*

J. C. Aznar, *Las artes e los pueblos de la España primitiva* (Madrid, 1954)

M. Almagro, A. Arribas, "El poblado y la necrópolis megaliticos de Los Millares (Santa Fé de Mondujar, Almería)," *Bibl. Praeh. Hispana* 3 (Madrid, 1963)

————, *Guia abreviada del Mus. Arq. de Barcelona* (Barcelona, 1954)

M. Boyle *et al.*, "Recollections of the Abbé Breuil," *Antiquity* 37 (1963), 12–18

H. Breuil, H. Obermeier, *The Cave of Altamira*[2] (Madrid, 1935)

————, P. Serrano Gomez, J. Cabré, "Les peintures rupestres d'Espagne IV: les abris del Bosque à Alpéra (Albacete)," *L'Anthropologie* 23 (1912), 529–561

G. E. Daniel, *Megalith Builders of Western Europe* (London, 1958), 59–75

————, J. D. Evans, "The Western Mediterranean," *Cambridge Ancient History*[2], Chap. 37 (1967), 46–39

J. Hawkes, *Prehistory and the Beginnings of Civilization* (London, 1963)

J. S. Koppa, W. Waldren, "Balearic Prehistory, a New Perspective," *Archaeology* 20 (1967)

G. and V. Leisner, "Die Megalithgräber der iberischen Halbinsel," *Madrider Forschungen* 1.1–3 (1956–1965); *Röm-Germ. Forsch.* 17 (1943)

J. Maringer, H. G. Bandi, *Art in the Ice Age* (New York, 1953)

L. Pericot, *La cueva de Parpalló* (Madrid, 1942)

A. do Paço, E. Sangmeister, "Citânia de Vila Nova de São Pedro," *Arq. e Hist.* 7 (Lisbon, 1956), 114 ff. Full bibliography in *Guia do Carmo* (Lisbon, 1961)

M. S. de Santuola, *Breves apuntes sobre algunos objectos prehistoricos de la provincia de Santander* (Santander, 1880; reprinted Madrid, 1964)

H. N. Savory, *Spain and Portugal: The Prehistory of the Iberian Peninsula,* (New York, 1968)

H. Schubart "Atalaia, uma necrópole da idade do bronze no Baixo Alentejo," *Archivo de Beja* 22 (1965)

J. de C. Serra Rafols, *Las Islas Baleares* (Barcelona, 1929)

O. da Verga Ferreira, "La culture du vase campaniforme au Portugal," *Mem. Serv. Geol. de Portugal* n. s. 6 (1966)

G. Zbyszewski, "L'Abbé H. Breuil et sa contribution à l'état de la préhistoire portugaise" (offprint; n.d.)

2 / Ships to Tarshish

M. Almagro, "El hallazgo de la ria de Huelva y el final de la Edad del Bronce en el Occidente de Europa," *Ampurias* 2 (1940), 85–143

M. Esteve Guerrera, "Excavaciones de Asta Regia, 1949–50, 1955–56," *Acta Archaeológica Hispanica* 3 (1962)

A. García y Bellido, *Fenicios y Carthaginienses en occidente* (Madrid, 1942), 230–292

———, *Iocosae Gades* (Madrid, 1951)

———, *La peninsula iberica en los comienzos de su historia* (Madrid, 1953), 146–166

E. Kukahn, A. Blanco, "El tesoro de El Carambolo," *Archivo Español de Arqueológia* 32 (1959), 38–49

J. Maluquer de Motes, "Nuevas orientaciones en la problema de Tartessos," *Primer Symposium de Prehistoria de la Peninsula Iberica 1959* (Pamplona, 1960), 273–297

J. R. Mélida, "Der Schatz von Aliseda," *Archäol. Anzeiger,* 1928, Sp. 497–510

H. G. Niemeyer, M. Pellicer, H. Schubart, "Eine Altpunische Kolonie an der Mündung des Rio Vélez," *AA,* 1964, Sp. 476–493

M. Pellicer Catalán, *Excavaciones en la necrópolis punica 'Lanrita' del Cerro de S. Cristobal (Almuñécar, Granada)* (Madrid, 1962)

L. Pericot, "Adolf Schulten, su vida y sus obras," *Anales de la Universidad de Barcelona: Memorias y Communicaciones* (1940), 45–76

J. Mᵃ· Soler Gracia, "El tesoro de Villena," *Excavaciones Arqueológicas en España* 36 (Madrid, 1965)

A. Vives, *Necrópolis de Ibiza* (Madrid, 1917)

3 / The Greeks in Spain

M. Almagro, *Inscripciones ampuritanas gregas, ibéricas y latinas* (Zaragoza, 1951)

———, "Excavaciones en la Palaeopolis de Ampurias," *Excavaciones Arqueológicas en España* 27 (1964)

———, *Ampurias: guia breve de las excavaciones y museo* (Barcelona, 1967)

R. Carpenter, *The Greeks in Spain* (Bryn Mawr, 1925)

J. A. Cean-Bermudez, *Sumario de las antigüedades que hay en España* (Madrid, 1832)

A. García y Bellido, op. cit., Chap. 2, 498–505
———, Hispania Graeca² (Barcelona, 1948)
N. Lamboglio, M. Almagro, "La estratigrafia del decumano A de Ampurias," Ampurias 21 (1959), 1–24
M. Oliva, "Las excavaciones en la ciudadela de Rosas," Noticiario Arqueológico Hispanico 6 (1962), 162–164
C. Sánchez-Albornaz, "Proceso de la romanizacion de España desde los Escipions hasta Augusto," Anales de historia antigua y medieval (Buenos Aires, 1949), 5–35
J. J. Van Nostrand, "Roman Spain" in Economic Survey of Ancient Rome 3 (Baltimore, 1937), 121–224

4 / The Iberian Resistance

A. Arribas, The Iberians (London, 1962)
A. Beltrán, "Azaila," IX Congreso Nacional de Arqueológia: Valladolid 1965 (Zaragoza, 1966), 308 ff.
J. Cabré Aguiló, Azaila (Barcelona, 1929)
———, "Azaila," Corpus Vasorum Hispanorum (Madrid, 1944)
M. Cardozo, "Die 'Castros' im Norden Portugals," Revista de Guimarães 69 (1959), 417–436
E. Cuadrado, "El Mundo Iberico: problema de la chronologia y de las in fluencias culturales externas," Primer Symposium de Prehistoria de la Peninsula Iberica 1959 (Pamplona, 1960), 252–253
A. García y Ballido, "Arte iberica," in R. Menendez Pidal, Historia de España I.3 (Madrid, 1954)
J. A. Gaya Nuño, Escultura iberica (Madrid, 1964)
M. Gomez-Moreno, "De epigrafia iberica," Revista Filologica Española 9 (1922), 341–366
———, "Sobre los Iberos y su lengua," Homenaje a Menendez-Pidal 3 (Madrid, 1925), 475–499
———, "La escritura iberica," Boletin de la Real Academia de Historia (1943), 251–278
C. F. C. Hawkes, report of excavations at Sabroso, Rev. de Guimarães 69 (1959), 521 ff.
A. Mendes Correia, "A Lusitânia pre-romana," in Damião Peres, Historia de Portugal 1 (Lisbon, 1928), 77 ff.
L. Michelena, "Comentarios en torno a la lengua iberica," Zephyrus 12 (1961), 6–23
M. Oliva, excavation reports on Ullastret, in Anales del Instito de Estudios Gerundenses 5 (1950) –16 (1963)
———, Ullastret, Guia de las excavaciones y su museo (Gerona, 1962)
———, Les Fouilles Archéologiques de l'oppidum d'Ullastret (Gérone, Espagne) (Gerona, 1963)
A. do Paço, "Citânia de Sanfins III; breve noticia de um tesouro monetario," Broteria 56 (1953), 673–689

———, "Citânia de Sanfins: intensité de sa romanisation," *IV Congreso Internacional de Ciencias prehistoricas y protohistoricas, Madrid 1954* (Zaragoza, 1956), 943–946

H. Schubart, "Die Iberer," in G. Lilliu, H. Schubart, *Frühe Randkulturen des Mittelmeerraumes* (Baden-Baden, 1967)

A. Tovar, *The Ancient Languages of Spain and Portugal* (New York, 1961)

A. Vasco Rodrigues, *Arqueológia da Peninsula Hispanica* (Porto, n.d. [ca. 1961])

5 / *Numantia's Last Stand*

G. Arias Bonet, "Cáceres el viejo guarda aun su secreto," *El Miliario Extravagante* 12 (Paris, 1966), 319–328

J. R. Mélida, "Excavaciones de Numancia," *Memorias de la Junta superior de exc. y Antigüedades* 1, 19, 31, 36, 49, 61, 74 (1916–1926)

A. Schulten, *Numantia*, 4 vols. (Munich, 1914–1931)

———, *Viriato* (Porto, 1940)

———, *Historia de Numancia*[2] (Barcelona, 1945)

———, "Ein römisches Lager aus dem Sertorianischen Kriege," *JbDAI* 33 (1918)

———, "Castra Caecilia: Erster Bericht," *AA* 1928, Sp. 1–14

———, "Castra Caecilia: Zweiter Bericht," *AA* 1930, Sp. 37–58

———, "Forschungen in Spanien 1928–1933," *AA* 1933, Sp. 513–566

———, *Sertorius* (Leipzig, 1926)

B. Taracena, *La ceramica iberica de Numancia* (Madrid, 1924)

F. Wattenberg, on 1963 excavations at Numantia, *Notic. Arq. Hisp.* 7 (1963), 132–142

6 / *From Caesar through Nerva*

A. Beltrán, "La muralla ciclopea de Tarragona," *Arqueologia megalitica y ciclopea Catalano-Balear* (Barcelona, 1965)

G. Bonsor, "Sketchbook of the Roman Necropolis at Carmona," *Hispanic Notes and Monographs* (New York, 1931)

A. D'Ors, *Epigraphía jurídica de la España romana* (Madrid, 1953), 167–280 (Lex Ursonis)

A. Floriáno, "Excavaciones en Mérida, campañas de 1934–36," *AEArq.* 17 (1944), 151–186

E. Garcia Sandoval, "Las casas Romanas de Mérida," *Exc. Arq. en Esp.* 44 (1966)

A. García y Bellido, *Cantabria romana* (Santander, 1952)

———, *Excavaciones en Julióbriga 1953–56* (Madrid, 1957)

E. G. Hardy, *Three Spanish Charters* (Oxford, 1912)

J. Hernandez Diaz *et al.*, *Catalogo arqueológico y artístico de la provincia de Sevilla* 2 (1943), 65 ff. (Carmona)

A. Hernandez Morales, *Julióbriga, ciudad romana en Cantabria* (Santander, 1946)

J. Heurgon, "La date des gobelets de Vicarello," *Revue des Études Anciennes* 54 (1952), 39–50

M. Macias, *Mérida monumental*² (Mérida, 1929)

J. R. Mélida, *Catalogo monumental de España: Provincia de Badajoz* (Madrid, 1925), 99–359 (Mérida)

Mᵃ· Angeles Mesquiriz de Catalan, *Terra sigillata hispanica*, 2 vols. (Valencia, 1961)

P. de Palol, *Guia arqueológica de Clunia* (Valladolid, 1961)

————, *Clunia Sulpicia* (Burgos, 1959)

P. Paris, *Promenades archéologiques en Espagne* 1 (Paris, 1910) (Osuna, Carmona)

A. Schulten, *Bilbilis, patria de Marcial* (Zaragoza, 1934)

————, *Tarraco* (Barcelona, 1948)

A. Sentenach y Cabañas, "Bilbilis," *Mem. Junta Sup. de Exc.* 3 (Madrid, 1918)

R. Thouvenot, "Bétique," *Bibliothèque de l'école français de Rome* 149 (Paris, 1940), 545–569 (Carmona)

7 / Spain Under the Spanish Emperors

M. Cardozo, "A proposito de lavra do ouro na provincia de Tras-os-Montes durante a epoca romana," *Rev. de Guimarães* 64 (1954), 113–141

————, "Das origens e técnica do trabalho do ouro e sua relação com a joalharia arcaica peninsular," *ibid.*, 67 (1957), 5–46

A. D'Ors, *op. cit.* above, 6 (Vipasca laws)

A. García y Bellido, "Colonia Aelia Augusta Italica," *Bibliotheca arqueológica* 2 (Madrid, 1960)

————, "Arquitectura en España durante la época romana," in R. Menéndez-Pidal, *Historia de España* 2³ (Madrid, 1962), 256–657

————, "L'Italica de Hadriano," *Les empereurs romains d'Espagne* (Paris, 1965), 7–26

G. Gosse, "Las minas y el arte minera de España en la antiguëdad," *Ampurias* 4 (1942), 43–68

W. Grünhagen, "Die Ausgrabungen des Terrassenheiligtums von Munigua," *Neue Deutsche Ausgrabungen in Mittelmeergebiet* (Berlin, 1959), 329–343

————, "Nuevos hallazgos de esculturas romanas en Munigua," *Arbor* (1961), 125–142

T. Hauschild, *Notic. Arq. Hisp.* 6 (1962) (Munigua baths)

N. Lewis, M. Reinhold, *Roman Civilization* 2 (New York, 1955), 188–194 (Lex metalli Vipascensis)

L. Monteagudo, "Restos romanos in España de interes turistico," Dirección general de promoción del Turismo, *Noticiario turistico*, Suppl. 193 (Madrid, 1966). (Roman mine-workings at Las Médulas de Carucedo)

T. A. Rickard, "The Mining of the Romans in Spain," *Journal of Roman Studies* 18 (1928), 129–143

R. Thouvenot, *op. cit.* above, 6. Index, s.v. Italica

M. Torres, "Instituciones economicas," in R. Menéndez-Pidal, *op. cit.*, 332–341 (Roman mines in Spain)

A. Viana, R. Freire de Andrade, O. da Veiga Ferreira, "A exploração das Minas de Aljustrel pelos Romanos," *Arquivo de Beja* 13 (1956), 3–19

8 / *Decline and Fall*

J. Alarcão, "On the Westernmost Road of the Roman Empire," *Archaeology* 26 (1967), 174–177 (Miróbriga, Cetóbriga)

A. Balil, "Colonia Iulia Augusta Paterna Barcino," *Bibl. Arq.* 4 (Madrid, 1964)

L. Chaves, "A Villa de Santa Vitória do Ameixial (Estremoz)," *O Arqueólogo Portugues* 30 (1956), 14–117

V. Corrcia, "Las mas recientes excavaciones romanas de interes en Portugal: la ciudad de Conímbriga," *AEA* 14 (1940–1941), 257–267

————, *Obras* 1 (Coimbra, 1946), 13–35 (reprint of lecture on Coimbra-Aeminium)

————, *Conímbriga* (Coimbra, 1956)

D. Fernando de Almeida, *Ruínas de Miróbriga dos Célticos* (Setubal, 1964)

A. Florensa Ferrer, *Las murallas romanas de la ciudad* (Barcelona, 1958)

A. García y Bellido, *Le Legion VII Gemina Pia Felix y los origenes de la ciudad* (Madrid, 1950)

E. Gibbon, *Decline and Fall of the Roman Empire* (London, 1776–1788), Chap. 40, II (on circus factions: Modern Library ed., Vol. 2, pp. 140–146)

M. Helleno, "A villa lusitano-romana de Torre de Palma (Monforte)," *OAP* n.s. 4 (1962), 313–338

N. Lewis, M. Reinhold, *op. cit.* above, 7, 230–232 (career of charioteer Diocles)

J. Marques da Costa, *Novos elementos para a localizacão de Cetóbriga* (Setubal, 1960)

P. Paris, G. Bonsor, "Exploration archéologique de Bolonia," *Annales de la Faculté des Lettres, Bordeaux, Bulletin hispanique*, 20 (1918), 77–127

————, "Fouilles de Belo," *Bibliothèque de l'Ecole des Hautes Etudes Hispaniques* 6–6 bis (Bordeaux-Paris, 1923–1926)

M. Pellicer, "Prospección arq. geofisica en Bolonia," *Notic. Arq. Hisp.* 7 (1965)

M. Ponsich, M. Tarradell, "Garum et industries antiques de salaison dans la Méditerranée occidental," *Bibl. éc. hautes ét. hisp.* 36 (Paris, 1965)

I. A. Richmond, "Town Walls in Hispania Citerior," *JRS* 21 (1931), 86 ff. (León, Lugo, Barcelona)

H. Schlunk, "Untersuchungen im frühchristlichen Mausoleum von Centcelles," *Neue deutsche Ausgrabungen* (Berlin, 1959), 344–365

B. Sparkes, rev. of Ponsich-Tarradell (above), *JRS* 56 (1966), 250–251

B. Taracena, "Las villas rusticas de España," *Investigacion y progreso* 15 (1944), 333–347 (Cuevas de Soria)

F. Udina Martorell, *Guia del Museo de historia de la ciudad* (Barcelona, 1963)

A. H. Weiss, "The Roman Walls of Barcelona," *Archaeology* 14 (1961), 188–197 .

Index